A
MIDWINTER
GOD

"Christine Valters Paintner's *A Midwinter God* brings her distinctive gift for creating a retreat in written form to a vital and important theme: finding the Divine presence in the midst of the dark seasons of our life. In doing this, she stands squarely in the tradition of the greatest Christian mystics, who taught that darkness, unknowing, and mystery can serve as profound initiations into spiritual healing and wisdom. This is a book to pray—and to savor."

Carl McColman

Author of *The New Big Book of Christian Mysticism*

"Paintner is a gentle and nurturing guide into the spiritual darkness that lies within each of us, encouraging us not to rush past our pain but to accept the invitation to dwell in its depths and find nourishment there. With thorough research, personal wisdom, and embodied practices, she leads us with compassion and curiosity into a midwinter that is warmed by the light of a loving God."

Cameron Bellm

Author of *A Consoling Embrace: Prayers for a Time of Pandemic*

"There is no shortage of spirituality books on overcoming difficult times, but there are perilous few that teach us how to look such times squarely in the face, trusting Wisdom to have her way. *A Midwinter God* is the latter, and what a gift it is. I absolutely loved this book."

Shannon K. Evans

Author and spirituality editor at *National Catholic Reporter*

A
MIDWINTER
GOD

Encountering the Divine in Seasons of Darkness

CHRISTINE VALTERS PAINTNER

SORIN BOOKS   Notre Dame, IN

© 2024 by Christine Valters Paintner

All rights reserved. No part of this book may be used or reproduced in any
manner whatsoever, except in the case of reprints in the context of reviews,
without written permission from Sorin Books®, P.O. Box 428, Notre Dame,
IN 46556-0428, 1-800-282-1865.

http://www.avemariapress.com/sorin-books

Paperback: ISBN-13 978-1-932057-29-4

E-book: ISBN-13 978-1-932057-30-0

Cover image © gettyimages.com.

Cover and text design by Brian C. Conley.

Printed and bound in the United States of America.

Library of Congress Cataloging-in-Publication Data is available.

I will give you the treasures of darkness and riches hidden in secret places.

—Isaiah 45:3

Contents

INTRODUCTION

God is not simply in the light, in the intelligible world, in the rational order. God is in the darkness, in the womb, in the Mother, in the chaos from which order comes . . . darkness is the womb of life.

–Dom Bede Griffiths

I first learned to love the darkness after my mother died. Not initially. At first, after holding her body close in those minutes after her last breath and then in the weeks that followed, I railed against the cold, black night of loss. I tried to send out a flare again and again. I once was a child of summertime, relishing the long days of brilliant sunshine and intense heat. I used to love the way summer would illuminate everything, making it seem filled with possibility.

Now I am a child of winter and moonlight. It was the only place where I could begin to weave the thread of my loss through my life with any meaning, where doubt and despair had a home and were welcomed to the table. Where faith is not an assumption but something wrestled with like the biblical story of Jacob in his long night with the angel. He walked away from that encounter blessed but limping. He would carry the sign of that struggle with him always.

Richard Rohr urges us to welcome the holy darkness, knowing that we most often will not go willingly into the "belly of the beast." It is only when darkness engulfs us through a great loss that we find ourselves compelled to embark on a journey we do not want. He writes, "As a culture, we have to be taught the language of descent. That is the great language of religion. It teaches us to enter willingly, trustingly, into the dark periods of life. These dark periods are good teachers. Religious energy is in the dark questions, seldom in the answers." We may try to find our way out by seeking answers, but it is the questions themselves that beckon us to an expanded vision. When we try to change or control what is happening, we are sidestepping the transformation that is possible. Rohr writes, "We must learn to stay with the pain of life, without answers, without conclusions, and some days without meaning. That is the path, the perilous dark path of true prayer."[1] This book is an invitation to enter the holy darkness.

What a courageous and powerful choice you have made to take this conscious path into the heart of midwinter. Darkness is, by its nature, an uncomfortable and uneasy place, but also a place of profound incubation and gestation, a source of tremendous and hard-wrought wisdom. If you feel some fear and trembling, this is a healthy response to a holy encounter.

We can gather resources to help sustain us in this experience of feeling unsettled, challenged, or pushed. Resources are anchors in the storms of our lives. Consider what accompanies you or steadies you on your way. Tools like grounding, being in nature, breathwork, placing your hand on your heart, holding a stone or prayer beads, or wrapping yourself in a prayer shawl or blanket can all be companions to support us as we make this journey. It is worth spending time considering what resources you have available to you and allowing yourself to feel connected and held. You will be invited to return to these regularly.

Nothing in our culture prepares us to deal with darkness and grief. We are told to cheer up and move on, to shop or drink our way to forgetting the pain we carry. Yet I believe, along with Rohr, that being faithful to our own dark moments is the path of true prayer. Our lives are filled with grief and loss. Everything is impermanent as the Buddhists say. Everything in this earthly existence passes away.

The path of holy darkness is a distinctly feminine way, feminine in the sense that we all contain feminine energies no matter our gender. The sacred masculine is concerned with light, ascension, and progress, while the sacred feminine embraces darkness, descent, and waiting. Both are essential to our spiritual journeys, but we tend to favor the former, and so we become off-balance.

My mother died twenty years ago. She had a serious chronic illness for many years, but her death was sudden and painful for me. I sat by her hospital bed those last five days of her life as she lay unconscious and attached to a web of tubes keeping her body alive by fighting the infection that had taken hold of her system.

The journey that followed was more painful than I had imagined. I was suddenly an orphan, no parents, no siblings, no children, and there was this confrontation with an existential aloneness that I think we all need to engage at some point in our lives. What I mourned more than anything was the absence of deeply rooted rituals to hold me in that space. I wanted to wrap myself in ancient prayers and traditions to help guide me through my grief and darkness. They existed but were not easily accessible. Even members of my church community wanted to rush me toward light and hope.

I believe that central to our spiritual path, we must hold the tension of lament and praise—we must learn the language of descent as Rohr says, as well as ascent. We need to allow ourselves to grow intimate with the contours of each. To praise without acknowledging our pain is a superficial and shallow response to the realities of the world in which we live. To lament without offering gratitude or praise is to unbind ourselves from hope and become mired in cynicism and despair.

The whole of the spiritual life is wrapped up in paradoxical tensions, which we must learn to live into rather than figure out. My mother's death was in many ways life-changing for me. I was confronted with questions and sorrow I had not known before. I was ushered toward a much more vibrant sense of my own mortality and the clarity that can accompany such a realization. The brilliance of autumn's colors reminds me of the way that death can bring the harshest kind of beauty, beauty that forces us to let go of what no longer serves us and embrace that which perhaps terrifies us most but we have always longed to do or be.

The significant losses of my life continue to echo through my being and shape who I am. I also believe we all carry grief that has gone unnamed and unmourned. Some of this is ancestral trauma, which presents as deep grief. Studies in the field of epigenetics show that the traumas of our ancestors ripple down to us. Epigenetics studies the way both behavior and environment can cause changes to your genes. The trauma your ancestors experienced is visible in your DNA. There are healing pathways that show us how to work with this trauma. Your ancestors experienced their own pathways through darkness.

My own multiple journeys through grief have demanded that I take the Midwinter God seriously. That I look her fiercely in the eye until I see the reflection of my own dread and stay with it, breathe through it, begin to enter it with curiosity to see what it has to teach me about living in meaningful ways, to even welcome it in with compassion and tenderness, to live a life of depth that takes seriously both suffering and joy. I am called to become friends with the thing I resist most—the inevitable loss of everything I love.

I love the darkness and the way it invites contemplation and rest, stillness and listening, awareness of the seeds planted deep within. I have been through the painful dark times as well, the times when the possibility of faith seemed far away, faith in myself, faith in God, faith in humanity. I have grieved deeply many times and dwelled in the ocean of sorrow, the night underworld. I know both the life-giving darkness and the painful darkness intimately. And yet, each time I have released into disintegration and been faithful to the journey, I have emerged with an even more profound and more mysterious sense of God. Grief and sorrow are fundamental parts of our lives and have much to teach us about our own potential for compassion and kindness. They enter us into solidarity with those who struggle with depression or a sense of meaninglessness in life.

As I walked winter mornings in the months following my mother's death, I became aware of the bareness of winter branches and the beauty of naked tree limbs dark against the sky. The questions of winter stirred in me. When I let go of all the embellishments of my life, what is the core that remains? What constitutes the bare bones of my life?

Often the process of release that winter calls us into—the surrender of ego and things and desires—can reveal, beneath all the foliage, a nest hidden in the branches. We suddenly discover, in the letting go, a place within that is nurturing the tender young life always unfolding anew. We journey toward the new birth, and sometimes it takes death for us to see it.

Winter reminds me that I know very little, that Mystery pulses through creation, through my own beating blood. It is the time to lay aside any easy answers offered by many religious stories and traditions that seek to assure me it will all be okay, so not to trouble myself. It is the season of humility. Some deaths bring relief, the laying down of the commitment that had become draining, the end of a relationship that had become destructive, the shedding of an identity that had become too narrow, or a long and painful illness finally ending. That relief is still accompanied by grief's draining sense of the familiar rushing out like blood pouring from a wound, the long, dark night of unknowing still ahead.

Overview of the Book

This book is divided into six chapters. In the first chapter, I begin with an appreciation for the gifts of winter and darkness and share more about how I came to the image of a Midwinter God.

In chapter 2, I explore the reality of spiritual bypassing and the ways we, understandably, try to avoid our difficult emotions by using spiritual concepts to bypass this experience.

Chapter 3 invites you into the landscape of grief and to see how grief is a reflection of how much we have loved in our lives.

Chapter 4 examines the *via negativa*, or way of unknowing in Christian mysticism, focusing on the teachings of Spanish mystic St. John of the Cross and the dark night of the soul.

Chapter 5 invites you to open to the compassionate and fierce dark feminine, which we encounter in Mary as the Mother of Sorrows and as the Black Madonna. We also explore briefly some of the dark goddesses of other cultures and the ancient story of Inanna, a Sumerian goddess who made a powerful journey of descent.

Chapter 6 explores three archetypes—the Orphan, the Destroyer, and the Sovereign—and how the journey into darkness asks us to embrace these aspects of ourselves so we might move from abandonment and a sense of victimhood to our disorientation and undoing and finally to a sense of empowerment. We also explore the descent of Persephone from Greek myth as an example of this journey. This is not a once-and-for-all journey but one we will be called to repeat many times throughout our lives.

As with most of my books, you are invited to enter into it as a retreat experience, rather than reading straight through. Each chapter follows a similar rhythm, beginning with a series of reflections on the theme. Then there is a reflection on a particular scripture passage written by my husband John. Following this is a meditation to help bring the teaching into your heart. Then I offer an expressive arts exploration, which is a series of invitations to process the material through creative expression. I explain more about these below. At the end of each chapter are some questions to help you reflect on what you have experienced. I close the chapter with some poems and writing from participants in previous online versions of this material when I led it as a retreat. I am deeply grateful to the many participants who opened their hearts to this journey and enriched my own writing and reflection.

Introduction to the Expressive Arts

Many of my books include creative practices and explorations to help readers integrate the materials. Reading is important; understanding is good. But to really embody and be transformed by what we read, we need to bring the materials and reflections into our hearts and bodies. To understand from a more intuitive place, from heart intelligence and wisdom of the flesh. This is especially true when it comes to navigating the dark. When we cultivate enough trust and allowing, our bodies, sensations, and emotions can become the site for allowing our experience to flow freely through us, rather than our habit of resisting and suppressing what feels uncomfortable.

For this reason, at the end of each chapter I invite you into an expressive arts experience, a "gush art" flow. This was a term coined by my colleague Sr. Jane Comerford when we worked together offering workshops in the expressive arts and spiritual direction. There are many phrases to describe it, but essentially it is a movement from one art form to another to deepen an experience.

I call these sequences of creative exploration "expressive arts unfolding." I use the word *unfolding* consciously as the focus here is on the process of what is happening within you as you engage in each creative act. You are not trying to create a beautiful product or figure something out. You do not want to control the direction of what happens. The gush in "gush art" refers to an experience of allowing images and feelings to flow through the various creative modalities. This is an act of prayer, and as such it is a surrender to the sacred movement of the Spirit within you as you pay attention.

Art helps us to make space for mystery, as it doesn't demand answers to our questions but helps us to rest in the tension. The expressive arts honors that moving from one art form to another often has a richer impact on our transformation than just engaging with one.

Use whatever materials you have available. This isn't about having the perfect supplies but about creating a sacred container that can hold your expression and exploration. Each chapter will follow a similar sequence, but feel free to change the order of things or leave parts out if you only have a short amount of time. Most of these sequences can be completed in about fifteen to twenty minutes, but if you only have five minutes on a given day, I encourage you to still enter into the creative space of unfolding by allowing some time to center, ponder the question, and then put on a piece of music to gently move, following the lead of your body.

Having a resourcing practice is really essential for this work. *Resourcing* means having various ways to return to a sense of safety in your body. These anchors might be a wonderful, cozy blanket you can wrap around yourself, or holding a stone that you love and feels good and solid in your hands. Prayer beads can also be a way to return to tactile connection as well as slow, deep breaths that can calm your nervous system. It is also important to make sure the space you are creating in feels safe. You can nurture this by closing your door and asking for privacy if you live with others, even locking the door if needed.

Following the opening sequence, if time and materials allow, I offer a suggestion for a visual art exploration, which might include gush art drawing (using colored pens, pencils, and markers to draw spontaneously; there are weeks exploring mosaic, collage, and altar-making as well) and a writing exploration based on the theme. Sometimes this is freewriting, where you write for five to ten minutes without letting your pen stop. Sometimes it is in response to a poem or my suggestion to try a specific poetic form. Most of all, I encourage you to have a spirit of playfulness in this process. You will likely also encounter deep grief in your body; let the grief and the playfulness dance together. You do not need to change how you are. Show up in the fullness of who you are, with the whole spectrum of feelings that are part of you.

At the end I always recommend resting into silence for a couple of minutes, which becomes a time of integration where we release words and images. Treat this time with reverence. Even if you feel tempted to rush through to a meaning, try not to analyze what has happened but let it gently ripen the way you might with a potent dream. The meanings will emerge gradually over time.

Expressive arts therapist Stephen K. Levine says that it is "essential to human beings to fall apart, to fragment, disintegrate, and to experience the despair that comes with a lack of wholeness." He goes on to write that it is at this moment of undoing that our creative spirits can guide the way. We have to let go of the old, rest into the darkness, and open ourselves to the new forms emerging. "*Poiesis*, the creative act, occurs as the death and re-birth of the soul. . . . The soul finds its form in art."[2] This is regardless of whether you consider yourself to be an "artist" or "creative." We were all born in the image of a Creator and all have the desire for expression in this way, whether through writing, art, dance, singing, gardening, cooking, or our work lives. This has nothing to do with making something "good" or something we can sell. This is the language of the soul finding form and expression in the world, which expands us in transformative ways.

Will you allow yourself to have moments of falling apart on this journey? To feel fragmented? Disintegrated? Will you allow yourself to experience the despair that arises from a lack of wholeness, even for a moment? Can you pause and simply notice your response to these invitations?

Art can be a lifeline in the midst of midwinter passages. The expressive arts focus on the power of the arts to heal and transform through paying attention to the *process* of creating rather than focusing on trying to create a beautiful product. Through the expressive arts we make space for whatever experience we are having, without trying to change it. Giving it form through poetry, art, or movement creates a safe and sacred container for expression. We aren't creating something to please another person; we are creating out of our raw emotion.

Psychologist Miriam Greenspan writes about how essential the expressive arts are for allowing the flow of our emotional life:

> Singing, chanting, and dancing are all forms of creativity that we can use to surrender to the flow of the dark emotions. Drum your anger, letting the beat release it. Sing your sorrow, letting the melody release it. Dance your despair, finding solace and new energy. Sculpt your fear, letting the emotions take shape in the clay. All of these creative outlets teach surrender to emotional flow, energize the bodymind together, and can be great fun! Creative flow is emotional surrender.[3]

Creating art is a way of giving form and outward expression to deeply felt inner experiences. Carl Jung believed that we come to new insight first through symbol and only later through verbalization. Cultivating a practice of creative expression offers a place in our lives to be with our preverbal experience and honor it. This is not meant to be great art but to be a container for inner expression of whatever you are experiencing, from grief to rage to joy to play. Welcome whatever comes without judgment. This can be for your eyes only. Writing is a wonderful way to follow the thread of our hearts into a richer understanding of what is happening inside of us.

I have found practices that reconnect me with my body to be very profound in my own healing journey. Often when we experience trauma, we disconnect from our bodies and emotions. We have memories and feelings frozen in our muscles that have not been expressed. Giving the body freedom to move gently or vigorously, as we feel led, in the ways it longs to is another way of honoring those experiences that have yet to be accompanied by words. Practices like yoga and expressive dance can help to heal the wounds of loss by giving us an experience of empowerment and strength. If you are unable to move physically in these ways, know that moving in your imagination can be powerful too. Always work within your physical, emotional, and spiritual limits. There is no need to push. Some of the most profound transformation emerges from gentle and slow movements.

Cultivating embodied awareness also includes the freedom to rest in stillness, as sometimes what the body needs most is to feel safe, held, and contained. Containment is a somatic principle that means having enough holding, safety, and grounding to allow strong emotions to flow without becoming overwhelmed or retraumatized. It is like having strong banks of a river to allow the water to flow through.

Therapist Gwen McHale writes:

> Containment is the capacity to stay present to and hold our experiences/emotions in such a way that they do not overwhelm or scare us. Without containment we feel out of control, emotions or thoughts threaten to bring us out of our depths. It can be terrifying.
>
> We need enough containment to provide banks to the river of our expression so we can stay in relationship to our experience, to ourselves, and not get washed away in the suffering.[4]

We learn the ability to contain for ourselves very early in life, needing another person to hold us and see us. When these needs are not met adequately, we then can experience a wide range of feelings, such as a sense of being overwhelmed, anxiety, fear, loneliness, and a lack of self-worth. Thankfully, science has discovered that the brain is plastic, meaning "it can change at any age. Old neural connections can be redirected and we can experience things in new ways. In other words healing is possible. We can learn to provide the holding and containment for ourselves that we did not experience as little ones and it is never too late to start feeling safe in the world."⁵ Seeking the companionship of a good therapist experienced in working with trauma can be very helpful in navigating this healing journey.

Ritual Space and Nature

We desperately need ritual spaces where lament can be expressed freely and fully, where we can cry out to God about the suffering we experience. We need meaningful rituals that help to mark our transitions into and out of the dark passage, honoring our courage in making a conscious journey and honoring our wisdom when we emerge. If you are going through a time of grief right now, I encourage you to create a daily ritual of lament. Designate a period—five to ten minutes is enough—to let yourself lament and give expression to your grief through sound, voice, body movement, tears, or whatever helps you to allow the grief to move through your body. You might begin and end with a way of resourcing yourself by finding something that comforts you or anchors you. Then choose a poem to read, or listen to the chime of a bell or a piece of music, to help create a container for this process and facilitate your expression of grief.

Forests and oceans remind us of our smallness; the humbling indifference of crashing waves or howling wind to our struggles can be a strange kind of solace, to be reminded that there are much bigger energies at work in the world. Spending time even with indoor plants or companion animals can connect us with the grounding energy of

Earth that helps to root us in life-giving ways. Daily walks (if you are able), observing the unfolding of the seasons, can bring us a profound wisdom and trust in the rise and fall, fullness and emptiness, of these natural cycles. This can be done also by looking out a window.

Working with This Book

I highly recommend reading this book with a friend, a spiritual director, or a small group. The journey into darkness can be demanding. It can make us uncomfortable and feel disoriented. Our resistance will kick in and we will come up with all kinds of reasons not to keep going. Resistance is all those parts of us that want to protect ourselves from harm. Sometimes it is wise to listen to these voices and rest, but sometimes we need to invite them to step aside. When we work with others, they can help us stay committed and discern the best path forward. They can support us in the tenderness we will likely unearth.

If a soul friend or group is not available to you, seek out a skilled mental health professional in these areas. Do not underestimate the power of the trees and mountains to also hold and companion you, as well as the love of all of the invisible ones across the veil, including angels, saints, and ancestors. Remind yourself each time you come to this work that you are not alone. Feel yourself held.

Questions for Reflection

- As you begin this process, what fears or reticence are you experiencing?
- Who are the soul friends you can call upon? If this relationship doesn't already exist for you, is there someone with whom you could cultivate this connection?
- What resources you? What makes you feel safe and supported? Consider tools, practices, places, people, animals, music, and other experiences and make a list to refer to when needed.

1

THE GIFTS OF WINTER AND DARKNESS

A major obstacle to creativity is wanting to be in the peak season of growth and generation at all times . . . but if we see the soul's journey as cyclical, like the seasons . . . then we can accept the reality that periods of despair or fallowness are like winter—a resting time that offers us a period of creative hibernation, purification, and regeneration that prepare us for the births of spring.

—Linda Leonard,
Call to Create: Celebrating Acts of Imagination

Western culture tends to worship the energies of spring and summer, with their abundance of light and growth, and reject the waning and fallow energies of autumn and winter. We are continually told to keep busy, to keep up, to get ahead, to achieve, to earn more money, to do more, to not let grief or other difficult emotions slow us down. Consequently, so many of us are exhausted and overwhelmed, depleted by trying to live the seasons of spring and summer all year long. The daylight world encourages us to fulfill our ambitions, to keep going, to push through any physical fatigue or pain. If this sounds like a familiar pattern to you, bring some deep compassion for yourself. This is the culture we swim in, and it can be challenging to live in a different way.

We find this in our churches, too, with an overemphasis on embracing the light and identifying darkness with evil. This is problematic on many levels, including the way it has been used to justify the oppression of people with darker skin and perpetuates racism. In her book *Learning to Walk in the Dark*, theologian Barbara Brown Taylor writes that theological language around darkness and light is quite problematic.

Everything that feels difficult or challenging is relegated to the dark, always in a battle with the light where God supposedly dwells. It also "implies things about dark-skinned people and sight-impaired people that are not true. Worst of all, it offers people of faith a giant closet in which they can store everything that threatens or frightens them without thinking too much about those things. It rewards them for their unconsciousness."[1]

Embracing the darkness as a site of sacred transformative potential demands that we become conscious of all the things we have pushed down into the night chambers of our being. It means surrendering our need to control everything under the bright light of analysis and understanding that we may initially be frightened by what we find. But it also means that we open ourselves to the wisdom of holy darkness.

Even during the night hours and winter season, artificial light illuminates our world, so we never fully rest into darkness. Whether the traffic lights, streetlights, emergency lights, bedside lamp, or our mobile phones and computer screens, unless we live rurally, we are unlikely to ever experience true darkness. We know that these lights throw off the rhythms of insects and animals and confuse birds on their migratory routes. The impact is widespread.

Writer Clark Strand points out that "we are addicted to light and all that it symbolizes—certainty, the supremacy of our own power and our own knowledge, even the belief that all things can be 'made clear.' Progress. Power. Perfection. Destiny."[2] Until relatively recently with the advent of electricity and the light bulb, our ancestors would have lived their lives governed by the rhythms of light and dark.

Autumn and winter are vital to the health of nature and to our own bodies. It is a time of releasing and letting go; the leaves that fall become compost for new growth later. It is a season that invites us to slow down and rest into the quiet, to welcome in the growing darkness, to listen to our dreams and to the mystery of it all.

While the Hebrew and Christian scriptures also at times reinforce the darkness and light dualism, there are texts that reveal a different face of the night. When Abraham is called to journey with Sarah to a new land, God tells him to count the stars in the sky, a distinctly night-time activity and central to Abraham's journey of trusting in the divine call. Later Jacob would have two significant dreams at night about angels: one where he sees them ascending and descending the rungs of a ladder to heaven, and the other when he wrestles what seems to be an angel all night. Because Jacob endures the entire night, he is blessed and given a new name. Jacob's son Joseph dreams significant dreams that then prompt the Pharoah's attention. Dreams play a significant role in the sacred texts, pointing to a profound source of night wisdom to be received in the darkness.

There is a rich mystical tradition of those seekers who knew the darkness as a place of holy encounter. When we embrace the dark, we meet the divine beyond our ordinary comprehension. We begin to see how all our images for God fall far short of the reality of the Holy One. There is tremendous wisdom in learning how to rest in the dark, to not resist its disorientation but see it as a sign of the numinous at work.

Paul Coutinho, SJ, writes in his book *Sacred Darkness*: "In darkness we experience God as God without making God in our own image and likeness. . . . Darkness actually purifies our vision—some of our anthropomorphic images of God slowly fade away. Then we can begin to experience God as God."[3] This can be an uncomfortable time of stripping away our familiar images of the divine, but ultimately it is in service of a much more expansive vision.

We begin our lives in the darkness of the womb, and all of creation emerged from the primordial darkness and emptiness. The first creation story of Genesis reads that when God began to create heaven and earth, "darkness covered the face of the deep" (Genesis 1:2). God pours out the divine essence into this darkness to create something splendorous in this union of light and dark.

In the Christian and Jewish traditions, the day actually begins the night before with the evening vigil. Jews also begin each month at the new moon or dark moon. In the Celtic calendar, the feast of Samhain on November 1, which corresponds to the Christian feasts of All Saints and All Souls, marks the start of the Celtic wheel of the year as the dark half of the year begins. In the Christian calendar, Advent, which begins in late November or early December, starts the new liturgical year at this time of descent into darkness in the northern hemisphere.

In monastic traditions, there is a practice of Compline, which is the night prayer where monks enter into the Great Silence, and vigils, where they arise in the middle of the night to chant and pray in the darkness. These early morning, before-dawn prayers meant they were still in the liminal space between sleeping and waking, a time of listening to the voice of the sacred in a different way than during daylight.

All of these practices are ritualized ways of honoring how darkness is the place where seeds start to germinate. We begin in the place of rest, not knowing what shape that seed will take. The oak tree, the butterfly, the swan, and the otter emerge from a sanctuary of darkness—from soil to chrysalis to egg to womb—which helps them to strengthen enough to emerge into the light of the world.

Perdita Finn, in her foreword to the book *Waking Up to the Dark*, writes:

> Seeds must settle into the soil before they unfurl. Black holes give birth to stars. We grow within the warm, pulsing darkness of our mothers' wombs, and are placed within the dark body of the earth when we die. Our lives are everywhere surrounded by darkness—the unknowable lives and times that came before us, the dark matter of the heavens and, always, our own inevitable deaths.[4]

Storyteller and mythologist Michael Meade, who lives in the Northwest, suggests that instead of the enlightenment, we now desperately need an "endarkenment."[5] This is a call to reclaim the power of fertile darkness in our lives, the gift of intuition and dreamtime, and the grace of rest and embodied knowing.

The Gifts of Winter

The time of winter and darkness does not follow a linear path. I won't be offering you a 1-2-3-step plan for getting through the dark. I will be offering you questions and invitations, wisdom from many of those who have made the journey before, practices that embrace unknowing and imperfection.

I will begin by sharing a bit more about how I came to this work specifically, since my sense is that you want a guide in this process who has traversed some of the landscape herself. While I still have a long way to go in this life in my continual unfolding and emerging, I have also learned a lot about anchoring myself and paying attention to my experience in the dark seasons of life.

This process really began for me in childhood and adolescence. I won't retell my entire memoir, but a brief sketch will give you a sense of the context of my life. I was raised in New York City where my father worked for the United Nations. He was originally from Latvia and Austria and my mother from the Boston area. I had the great privilege of attending an excellent school and traveling widely in our summers as a family. But there was a dark shadow side to our family life. My father was an alcoholic, compulsive gambler, and sex addict. His addictions worsened as I entered my adolescence, and he was hospitalized three times for detox when he became delusional.

In the month of June, on my twenty-fifth birthday, he left me a nasty phone message; we had been growing further apart since my marriage the year before. I wrote a long-overdue letter to him, stating that I could no longer be in communication with him when he was being so abusive. I got a letter in reply that Christmas expressing his deep disappointment in me. The following March 6, he died suddenly of a heart attack. We hadn't spoken in the previous nine months except for the letter we each sent.

I was honestly relieved when he died. My parents had separated, but now my mother was fully free of my father's emotional abuse and taken care of for the rest of her life through his pension. I felt as if I had grieved for his loss many times, so when his death did come, I mostly felt glad. Many people might feel guilt in acknowledging this reality, but I have come to realize that it is not uncommon. Death brings a multitude of conflicting feelings.

In my early twenties, I also developed a serious autoimmune condition—rheumatoid arthritis—which my mother had already suffered with for many years, and it had ravaged her body. I had many periods of struggle with my body, especially in the early years of my illness before medications improved, and I continue to experience shifting body limitations thirty years on.

Eight years after my father's death, my mother died suddenly. She went into the ICU with a staph infection in her bloodstream and was unconscious. I sat vigil with her and, two days later, made the extraordinarily painful decision to take her off life support. As an only child, it was my choice to make. She died three days after that in late October.

I count that moment as the time I was really thrust into darkness as a conscious journey (rather than the previous painful periods I was desperately trying to flee). This is where the image of the Midwinter God first emerged for me—on long walks among bare branches through those cold winter months following my mother's death. I found the spareness of winter a comfort and source of solace. Among the trees, I didn't have to pretend I was doing okay; I didn't have to take care of others who couldn't stand to be around my grief. I wailed in sorrow at the loss of my mother. I railed in anger at the betrayals of my father.

As I moved through fall and into winter, I discovered that the world around me was mirroring something about my grief back to me. When I walked, I felt as if the trees I loved so much in our neighborhood park were bearing witness to the journey of release, of stripping away, and of moving deep into a place of barrenness and solitude that I was experiencing as a part of my own grieving journey.

Once the last leaf had surrendered its futile grip and drifted gently to the ground, I was propelled into winter. Bare branches. Days that grew shorter. The sun, when it was visible, dipped low along the horizon, so even in daytime there was a darkness that lingered and pressed upon my imagination.

The autumn walks that provided me such solace in their beauty, in winter were now times to look even more deeply for signs of life around me. Rain drizzled and doused and poured in fits and starts. In the midst of my deep ache and longing for a sense of lightness, I witnessed the subtle slow waves of velvety moss that spread up tree trunks and across sidewalks. I once heard a saying on National Public Radio, while living in Seattle, that in the Northwest if moss isn't growing on your north side, you are moving too fast. I shared this with the driver of an airport shuttle as we made our way through blankets of thick rain. "You can tell an outsider made that up," he responded, "because around here moss grows on *all* sides." And it was true; I began to discover moss everywhere that winter and fell in love with its green, persistent hope while also staying present to the aches that consumed me.

Gradually I became overwhelmed by fatigue, headaches, and depression brought on by grief over my mother, and I began to search for treatments to soothe my ills: light boxes, yoga, craniosacral therapy, Prozac, Celexa, Wellbutrin, long walks, short walks, chiropractic work, deep breathing, biofeedback, meditation, massage, magnesium, vitamin B, rhodiola, fish oil, green smoothies, blood-type diets, allergy diets, and more. One treatment after another became like moving the beads on an abacus, creating my own mathematics of healing—if I only tried enough therapies, something would *have* to help. Something would lift this weight that had wrapped itself around me.

One drizzly morning, I quite reluctantly entered the small dark living room of a psychic. At this point, I was willing to try anything. She answered the door in faded jeans and an old cream-colored sweater, blowing her nose because of a bad cold. Not exactly the crystal ball and cascade of silk scarves I had imagined. Yet, despite the fact that I had told her nothing about myself except for my name, she gently began by saying, "I sense great sadness over your mother." I started to cry tears from places I didn't know even existed inside of me. I thought I had cried deeply already, but they were just streams and tributaries I had waded through. Here was the great river of my grief sweeping me up in its current. I would have to swim.

We live in a very summer-oriented culture. We value perpetual productivity and fruitfulness. And yet living this kind of energy all year drives us to burnout and depletes our bodies. It drives us to suppress grief over very real losses. Winter offers an invitation into a space of contemplation and rest, of incubation and mystery.

Part of the journey into embracing winter is to honor our needs in navigating these seasons. I want to add a note here for those who suffer from seasonal affective disorder. This is a very real condition where a person is impacted in significant physical and emotional ways by the reduction of light in the winter. This is something that needs to be treated with kindness and gentleness, and often with medical intervention. We don't think our way out of it, so please make sure to get treatment if needed, especially from a qualified mental health professional. Compassion for ourselves is always primary. We always go gently with all of our tenderness.

In my own process of healing from grief, I discovered the wisdom and depth of winter. I have learned to love it on its own terms—not just as a preparation and precursor for spring's blooming but for all the ways it calls me deeper into rest and unknowing. Being fully awake and conscious in the dark days of winter can be challenging. Unknowing and mystery are often uncomfortable and radically disorienting experiences. We have all had winter seasons in our lives when what was familiar was stripped away, when we had to hold grief and open ourselves to the grace of being rather than doing. Winter calls us to trust that fallowness and hibernation are essential to our own wholeness.

As someone with an autoimmune illness that causes tremendous fatigue and pain at times, I found that winter also became an invitation to lay down my busyness and striving and honor my body's deep need for rest. I came to see how autumn and winter are really the seasons of the contemplative and the monk—stripping away, releasing, letting go, descending, resting, incubating, and being. Not everyone has the capacity, in terms of space and time, to dive fully into the invitations of the winter season; however, even a few minutes a day of honoring this reality can make a difference and create an internal shift.

The spiritual journey is not about growing more certain about the world but about embracing more and more the mystery at the heart of everything. In a world where so many people are so very certain about the nature of things, especially in religious circles, about whom God includes and excludes, I believe unknowing calls us to a radical humility. As we mature, we must engage with what our own mortality means for us, knowing that we will one day enter what I call the Great Unknowing, the final threshold of our lives. The season of winter helps us to practice for this.

In his book *The Soul of the Night*, religious naturalist Chet Raymo describes our relationship to darkness and silence:

> There is a tendency for us to flee from the wild silence and the wild dark, to pack up our gods and hunker down behind city walls, to turn the gods into idols, to kowtow before them and approach their precincts only in the official robes of office. And when we are in the temples, then who will hear the voice crying in the wilderness? Who will hear the reed shaken by the wind?[6]

This is a call to step out into the night, to embrace the winter, to listen closely to the wild silence shimmering through the darkness and see what new things we hear when we release our need to have everything figured out, including God. Winter invites holding this paradox of the clarity that comes with seeing what is most important in your life and the unknowing that comes with engaging deeply with mystery. Again, resourcing yourself and connecting with a close friend, or to the presence of nature and the angels, saints, and ancestors who reach out toward us in love, can really help us tolerate the disorientation and discomfort of being in this liminal space. Ritual, containment, and resourcing are key to helping us stay present to our experience.

I have come to believe that this is in part what I am called to in life—to continue on my own conscious path of descent and to create spaces to gather others who want to know there is an alternate way of being to the culture of "cheer up and get on with it." To gather those who rush to fill their days with endless tasks in an unconscious effort to avoid being present to their inner lives and all that might be calling to them under the noise and busyness.

I believe at heart that these winter experiences of loss are initiations into something deeper and more profound. This is not to say that we are somehow "given" these experiences to learn a particular "lesson" in life. I refuse to ever assign such glib intentions to how the universe works. But the fact is that when we gather in community, when we have wise elders and mentors to guide us on the way, and when we allow those traveling through the darkness to be seen and heard and witnessed, these passages can become holy ways. They become portals to deeper meaning. The God I believe in does not give us suffering but companions us intimately through it, offering the possibility of transformation.

My mother's death was in 2003. I was very blessed to eventually walk into the office of a Jungian analyst who has been a companion to me on this journey in the many years since. I count his wise presence in my life as one of the great gifts, someone who would sit with me and ask me to continue deeper into the dark passageways of my interior, never asking me to cheer up or move on. I learned to become curious about, rather than fearful of, the dark. I brought compassion to all of my hurting places rather than resisting and rejecting them.

This is just a small part of my story, but I offer it to you as a context for my own love of winter and my passion for continuing to explore its riches while also finding myself trembling again and again in its wake.

When contemplating the dark night of the soul, it is essential to have others in our lives who can be with us. We ultimately always take the journey alone, but to know there is a soul friend, a wise spiritual director, or a therapist who will stay with us, help to witness our experience, is so important. I encourage you to consider who in your life can help to offer you this support. Who gives you permission to be wherever you are, without rushing you toward resolution or light? Treasure this person and cultivate your relationship in the coming season as you integrate what you read in these pages.

In this first chapter, we are just beginning to break open the gifts of winter. Winter invites us into mystery, unknowing, and fallowness. It calls us to remember the fertile darkness and to have faith in night's power and possibility. It asks us to treasure dreamtime. We will be exploring the harder facets of winter as well: the wrenching pain, the stripping away of all that comforts, and the deep ache in our bones. In this journey toward reclaiming the gifts of winter and staying present, much is demanded of us. It requires endurance, presence, and a deepening trust in the cycles of things.

The Spiritual Practice of Being Uncomfortable

One of the greatest gifts of the seasons to me as a writer and artist is the profound wisdom of cycles, how everything rises and falls and then rises again. When we are in a dry spell, we may panic because the words or inspiration seems absent, but often it is a fallow time, a wintertime of the soul to enter into some rest both inward and outward and to allow time for the seeds to sprout again.

In a culture that demands continual productivity, there is no room to honor these natural rhythms, and we may begin to believe that our worth is determined by how much we can produce, how many books or paintings or workshops we can create, or whatever it is that tugs at you. I sometimes wonder if all the "creativity" titles that have been published in recent years feed into this phenomenon, offering valuable inspiration but forgetting to honor the rhythm of the creative process. Yet, the winter periods will come. We can expend lots of energy resisting them at every turn, trying to keep producing, or we can gently surrender into them, listening attentively for spring budding.

The monastic Liturgy of the Hours of the day offers similar wisdom as the seasons, the rise and fall of each day from sleeping to waking and sleeping again. There is a time for awakening and rising and embracing the work of the day. There is a time for slumber and dreams and renewal. I love the images of gestation, emptiness, hibernation, purification, and regeneration. I invite you to ponder these gifts and invitations. Winter summons us to a place of deep rest.

Part of my daily contemplative practice these last few years has been yin yoga. In yin yoga, the poses are held for long periods of time (anywhere from three to twenty minutes). The physical effect is a stretching of the connective tissue of the joints. The spiritual invitation is to go to the edge of my discomfort and rest there, staying present to my experience over time, to soften into the edges and continue to breathe. Each morning I willingly go into uncomfortable places to practice being at these edges of life. Slowly the tissues soften and I am able to drop further into my body.

There are many parallels between the wisdom of the Desert Mothers and Fathers and the path of yin yoga. These wise elders went out into the desert, the place of barrenness where life is stripped bare, and they sat with their discomfort, paying attention to their inner experience. In this wild space, they confronted their inner voices, the temptations, the distractions, and the tyranny of thoughts that would arise. They kept showing up until they could begin to cultivate a sense of equanimity. They were seeking *hesychia*, which is the Greek word for stillness. It means more than silence or peacefulness; there is a sense in which the stillness is the deep, shimmering presence of the holy. They knew of the path of emptying, of being stripped away to one's essence, of releasing all of our certainties. Silence is the appropriate response to the great Mystery of life.

These wise monks teach us that we are called to stay awake to the full spectrum of our experience and stay present to what is happening inside of us. This is the practice of a lifetime, and we will find ourselves again and again engaged in our favorite methods of self-numbing and distraction. Among these is dissociation, an experience of detachment from your body or the world, or a sense that things aren't real. This coping mechanism can be very helpful, especially when our system is overwhelmed. However, aspects of dissociation, especially when they get in the way of us living the life we desire for ourselves, can be unhelpful or even problematic. If this is familiar to you, I invite you to become curious about how this shows up for you. What resourcing helps you to stay present, even for a few seconds?

Widening Our Threshold of Tolerance

We each have a threshold of tolerance for uncomfortable or painful experiences. When we stay within this range, we can be present to what life brings us in the moment. When we drop below our threshold, we become numb to what is happening and seek out things that help us avoid the pain, like drugs or overwork. When we move above the threshold, our anxiety kicks into overdrive and we feel panicked, unsettled, or ill at ease.

The only way to widen our threshold of tolerance is to slowly and gently dance at its edges, to consciously go to uncomfortable places and stay present. When we risk the unfamiliar, our resilience grows, and we become more capable of living life fully. Again, it is vital to have a resource and sense of relative safety to begin to explore this territory. Allow time to anchor yourself with something that comforts you, before approaching what might be uncomfortable.

In one of the sayings of the Desert Fathers and Mothers, a monk comes to visit Abba Moses and asks him for a word. The reply he received was "Go sit in your cell, and your cell will teach you everything." The monastic cell is a central concept in the spirituality of the desert elders. The outer cell is really a metaphor for the inner cell, a symbol of the deep soul work we are called to, to become fully awake. It is the place where we come into full presence with ourselves and all of our inner voices, emotions, and challenges, and are called to not abandon ourselves through anxiety, distraction, or numbing in the process. It is also the place where we encounter God deep in our own hearts.

Connected to the concept of the cell is the cultivation of patience. The Greek word is *hupomone*, which essentially means to stay with whatever is happening. This is similar to the central Benedictine concept of stability, which on one level calls monks to a lifetime commitment with a particular community. On a deeper level, the call is to not run away when things become challenging. Stability demands that we stay with difficult experiences and stay present to the discomfort they create in us.

In 2010, the year I turned forty, I flew to Vienna for some time of retreat. It is an ancestral place of the heart for me. A few days after I landed, I developed symptoms of a blood clot and went to the emergency room. I was examined by the doctor who told me there were several tests they would run and that I needed to stay in a wheelchair and not move about at all because the clot could move to my heart or brain and cause instant death.

I was there in a foreign hospital alone, and for eight hours, my wheelchair became my monastic cell, the place where I practiced full presence to my inner life as best as I could. I witnessed my mind moving between different states: feeling terrified that I could die at any moment, feeling curious about how I experienced the possibility of dying sooner than I expected, feeling disconnected from the reality of the experience, noticing my internal responses to getting test results, having moments of deep peace, and of course, having times when my mind would move to distractions as a way of avoiding the whole process.

It ended up being a profound, while also traumatic, experience for me, and I was so grateful for monastic wisdom and contemplative practice to carry me through those dark moments. I am also profoundly grateful to be alive. In the years that followed, much of my sense of security and certainty about life and the ways I try to control things were stripped away, which has been profoundly freeing. I was thrust to the edges of my threshold and, by staying present, have discovered a wider landscape within me. This experience was a significant seed for my husband and I eventually moving to Europe two years later— the sense that my time in this world was not forever and that I should follow my heart's longings where they led me.

We don't need to travel long journeys to grow in the spiritual life. Wherever we are, we are called to stay in the monk's cell, which means to stay present to our experience. As a culture, we rarely acknowledge the value of being uncomfortable. We strongly discourage people who are grieving to stay with their sadness but instead tell them to "cheer up" or "move on" rather than explore what grief has to teach them. We are forever seeking the next thing to make us feel good.

So much of what passes for spirituality these days is about making us happy, about affirmations and having positive experiences. We engage in what the fourteenth-century Sufi poet Hafiz calls "teacup talk of God," where God is genteel and delicate. Sometimes we really need this; we need to remember that we are good and beautiful and whole just as we are.

But sometimes we need to be uncomfortable. Sometimes we need to remember a God of wildness who calls us beyond our edges to a landscape where we might discover a passion and vitality we never knew we could experience. We may cultivate a freedom we have never known before because our fears become something to move toward rather than away from. Developing the capacity to endure and remain open to difficult feelings is part of the movement toward spiritual maturity.

In my own life, I practice this daily through yin yoga, journal writing, movement, and meditation, and by staying as present as I can to experiences life inevitably thrusts upon me, seeking to dance at my own edges, to move toward the risky places. By staying present to the discomfort of life, we grow in our resilience and our ability to recover from the deep wounds that life will offer us again and again. We grow in our compassion for ourselves as we learn to embrace all of the vulnerable places within. This includes the parts of ourselves that disconnect or want to run away as well. This is the radical hospitality of biblical and monastic tradition. And as we embrace these in ourselves, we grow in our compassion for one another. We grow in our ability to experience *hesychia*—that deep presence and peace—in the midst of life's messiness and uncertainty.

Several years ago, I participated in a powerful retreat based on BodySoul Rhythms, which was developed by Marion Woodman, a Jungian analyst, along with two expressive arts therapists. Sherry

Wheaton, who was one of the facilitators of the retreat, offered this image of how dancing at the edges of our comfort helps to widen this threshold and expand our resilience. Then when life throws us into a place where we would normally get very anxious or numb ourselves, we have developed the capacity to stay more present to our experience. We might respond to life with more equanimity. We can also offer this gift to others by not responding with anxiety to their challenging stories.

I do think much of spiritual writing today focuses more on what makes us feel good and secure in our theological frameworks. There is certainly a place for this, but there is much to be said for walking toward what makes us uncomfortable in service of widening our own capacity to meet discomfort. The God who calls us beyond our edges is often a fierce presence, creating a healthy sense of awe and trembling. We hold these in loving tension. It is perhaps the masculine face of God that invites these growth edges, but the feminine face provides us the grounding, the resourcing, the transformative cocoon, and the community to enable us to bear the journey of growth.

Scripture Reflection by John Valters Paintner

Sabbatical Year and Sabbath

> *For six years you shall sow your land and gather in its yield; but the seventh year you shall let it rest and lie fallow, so that the poor of your people may eat; and what they leave the wild animals may eat. You shall do the same with your vineyard, and with your olive orchard. Six days you shall do your work, but on the seventh day you shall rest. (Exodus 23:10–12)*

This section of the book of Exodus begins back in chapter 19 when the Israelites reach Mount Sinai to formalize the covenant. This is shortly after Yahweh had rescued the Israelites from slavery and saved them from a number of difficult situations in the wilderness by providing food, water, and medical care. The people are grateful (although that is after a not insignificant amount of complaining on their part) but in need of a bit of guidance. After generations of oppression, they aren't exactly sure where to go or what to do. And so God offers an arrangement, a formal contract. Yahweh will continue to be their God if they agree to be God's People. Moses even provides a written list of instructions that spells out their role in this relationship, beginning with the Ten Commandments he receives in chapter 20.

While most people seem to focus solely on these ten laws, they aren't even the only commandments in this chapter. There is some minor disagreement about the way the commandments are divided, but the Jewish tradition on the matter is that there are 613 commandments in total in Exodus.

Modern audiences tend to ignore the other 603 for a variety of reasons. Or perhaps worse, people will cherry-pick commandments to support their own personal causes or agendas. These tend to be either political in nature (attacking the "sins" of others while ignoring one's own shortcomings) or attacking religion in general as being too ancient or out of touch with modern sensibilities. We need to find a balance between not judging an ancient culture too harshly and not being completely beholden to ancient practices through a deeper understanding of the full context and history of the text.

Chapter 22 continues with more laws about restitution when an injustice happens, because society can be messy; there will inevitably be some conflict when lots of people live in proximity to one another. The chapter ends with a hodgepodge of laws covering everything from banning female sorcerers to caring for immigrants to not charging interest on borrowed money. Chapter 23 begins in the same vein with a collection of seemingly unrelated laws that in fact share a common focus of equal justice under the law.

But that brings us to our passage under consideration about keeping the Sabbath holy. Like other verses in this section and elsewhere in the Bible, some commandments seem to be an extension or further explanation of previous commandments (even ones found in the original Ten Commandments). Here, the personal ban on working one day in every seven is extended to the land itself. The people are told to let their fields lie fallow one year in every seven. The poor—those without land or family (and animals)—are allowed to eat the wild harvest.

Our theme for this chapter is the gifts of winter and darkness. This commandment is obviously not just a season. However, both it and the original weekly Sabbath point to the necessity of rest. I hesitate to use the word *useful* here because rest is good in and of itself. It doesn't have value only because it might help recharge one's batteries to be more productive. That's a sneaky trap of our modern society, where even rest and relaxation are seen as subservient to the goal of constant productivity.

Rest is a good thing. It is a needed thing, even when it doesn't lead to anything else. Because without it, humans break down. Entire ecosystems (natural and cultivated) eventually grind to a halt.

Judaism can offer advice on a realignment of our thinking. Traditionally, Sabbath isn't seen as a break from work. Rather, work is seen as part of the preparation for the Sabbath. It is the culmination and goal of our endeavors. Sabbath is not just the most important thing; it is the only important thing. Whether it is weekly or yearly, Sabbath is a moment outside of time. It is the eternal now that is not worried about the past or anxious about the future; it is just now, the moment that is. Sabbath is not just a glimpse of heaven to come but also the kingdom of God here and now. That is its great beauty and blessing.

How can you embrace the season of winter and darkness for its own sake?

Meditation

Finding Support Within

I invite you to connect to a place of sanctuary within yourself. One of the tools that can be a real gift when we're doing this work is knowing that we have within us the resources we need to steady us, to ground us, to keep us centered, and to keep us calm during whatever it is we're experiencing. If at any point in this meditation, or during any other exploration I invite you into, there is too much activation in your body, see if you can find a resource around you that connects you to your heart. For example, this might be an object like a flower or a statue, a blanket, or a view out your window.

Take a few more nice deep breaths. As you breathe this time, first become aware of your body. Notice if there's any place of holding or tightness. See if you can be really gentle and compassionate with your-self. Another invitation I will give to you over and over again in this journey is to offer yourself the gift of compassion and gentleness on all levels. If there's any place where you feel discomfort or pain or holding, see if you might bring your breath there, offer some gentle softening, and bring some compassion. Drop your awareness into your heart center again. Let go of any need to figure things out or get things done. Allow yourself to be present here in this sanctuary of the heart. Become aware of anything that you're feeling right now and allow yourself to be just as you are without the need to change anything.

Offer a loving welcome to whatever you're feeling. There might be anxiety or grief or trepidation, there might be joyfulness or anticipation, or there might be a mix of these things. Honor that each of us is a gathering of many parts. We don't have to feel one way in any given moment and hold the fullness of who we are. Welcome in whatever is true for you. Connect to the sanctuary of the heart, where we encounter the Beloved, the Sacred Source, using whatever name you use to call on that reality that the mystics talk about, the infinite source of com-passion, the living flame of love. They all tell us the same thing: that in our hearts is the spark of this divine presence that burns in each of us no matter who we are or what we've done. That essential wholeness is always a part of us. Rest into that sanctuary of the heart and call on the infinite source of compassion. See what name you want to give for that presence in your life, in your heart. Maybe it is a name that you already use or maybe there's a new name for the divine you are being invited to consider. Rest for a few moments.

In the sanctuary of the heart, there is nothing that we have to do. This is a place of pure presence, of pure being as opposed to doing. We can rest into this interior place and take a deep breath. Soften everything, release your grasping, release your need to figure things out, and release your need to be anywhere else on the journey than where you are right now. Draw from that infinite compassion to fill our hearts and to fill our bodies and our beings and to know that presence as a gift and a resource in our lives, a way of being in the world that is deeply rooted and connected to love, even in the moments when it feels really hard to do that or to remember that. Know that if, each day, you spent a couple of minutes connecting to this sanctuary of the heart and to this loving presence, you might feel that consistent quality and steadiness in more of the moments of your life.

Then, open your imagination to the divine presence who wants to reflect something in you back to you. This part of ourselves we sometimes call the inner witness, sometimes the true self. It might be other names, our divine essence. It's the part of ourselves that can behold everything that's happening within us from a calm, centered, and compassionate place. We cultivate this presence within us through meditation practice and through other forms of mindful awareness.

Any time you feel you're starting to get swept away in anxiety or fear, or the grief feels overwhelming, call on this divine presence and also call on this part of yourself. It can also help to have something tangible that represents this divine essence for you, that externalizes it, something you can touch and hold, such as prayer beads or an icon or a stone.

The paradox here is that the deepest part of yourself is the reflection of the divine. This part of yourself can welcome in whatever comes and hold it with love. Rest into that presence, whether this is an old familiar friend or whether this is a part of yourself that you're just beginning to come into relationship with. Offer a few moments of presence, of acknowledgment, with a sense of how it feels in your body and in your spirit, when you rest into this inner witness.

Take a couple more deep breaths and imagine that you're offering a little bow to this source of divine love within you. You're offering a bow to your inner witness, the calm, centered, compassionate guide within your heart and to this interior, to this sanctuary space. Know that you can return in these coming days, as I hope you will, over and over again and, with this infinite presence, connect with your inner witness and know them both as primary companions with the midwinter journey. Take three really slow, deep breaths, and very gently come back to the room that you're in.

Creative Exploration

Expressive Arts Unfolding

In each chapter, I will suggest a similar sequence of expressive arts explorations to follow to allow space for you to honor whatever is unfolding. Art helps us to make space for mystery as it doesn't demand answers to our questions but helps us to rest in the tension. The expressive arts honor that moving from one art form to another often has a richer impact on our transformation than just resting with one.

Use whatever materials you have available. This isn't about having the perfect supplies but about creating a sacred container that can hold your expression and exploration. Each chapter will follow a similar sequence, with creative prompts reflective of the theme, but feel free to change the order of things or follow your own intuition.

You will want to have a journal, a pen, plain paper, and some crayons, colored pencils, or markers available.

Time limits can create a sense of containment. This sequence can be completed in fifteen to twenty minutes.

Centering
Begin with centering. Connect to your breath. Allow your breath to bring your awareness down to your heart (one to two minutes).

Plant the Seed with Some Questions
- What is my relationship to the season of winter like?
- Where do I experience resistance?
- What are the gifts I want to embrace?

Connect to Your Body
Find a meditative piece of music and become present to your body's wisdom and longing. How does your body want to move today? What would feel really good and delicious? You might move just one of your hands or bring your whole body into the movement, or anywhere in between. Work with your body's needs. Find patterns of movement that feel wonderful and repeat them a few times, savoring the experience. This is a time to explore what would nourish your body and help it to experience more ease. This is a form of resourcing ourselves through pleasure and joy. When the song is complete, rest for a few moments in stillness and just notice the energy in your body moving and how it feels.

If there is a different experience present, for example, some physical or emotional pain, you are invited to also see what is needed in response. This might involve moving with it or resting, as your body desires. You are always welcome to engage this practice in your imagination if moving in any way feels like too much.

Gush Art Drawing
Pick up colors that call to you and draw lines, shapes, and symbols in whatever way feels satisfying. Let yourself draw like a child, without concern for making great art. Open yourself to some playfulness in the experience if that feels accessible to you. When your thinking mind

enters with all of its judgments, release them as much as possible and try to return to the present moment.

Call to heart the opening question. See what wants to emerge in response.

Allow five minutes for this. You might want to set a timer and see if that helps create a container for you. Or you can keep drawing until you feel done.

Writing Exploration: Beginning

Turn to your journal and write about what you are noticing. This isn't a time for analysis but a time for curiosity, inquiry, and discovery. What is emerging in movement and color? What feelings are arising? What memories or images feel important?

What is your intention for this time of exploration through this book? What is the prayer you offer as we begin? Consider writing a short prayer to bless this journey and memorizing it or write it somewhere you will see it regularly so that you have it available to you as we move through the explorations.

Silence

At the end, allow one to two minutes to rest into silence, letting go of all the words and images that have come. This is a time of integration, allowing your body and soul to integrate what has been stirred up in the process.

Treat this time with reverence. Try not to analyze what has happened, but let it gently ripen over time the way you might with a potent dream. The meanings will emerge gradually over time.

Questions for Reflection

- What are the experiences in your life that have brought you to this book?
- What wisdom have you already discovered about navigating the midwinter way?

- What do you find most challenging about staying present to winter in your own experience and in offering a compassionate presence to others?
- Where in your life right now do you need the healing renewal of the long winter nights?
- What happens to you when you don't allow periods of fallowness in your life?
- How might you honor the winter season in even the smallest of ways each day?
- When you are in the midst of a time of darkness and midwinter, do you scramble to make meaning from the experience?
- Can you rest in the space of feeling undone, unraveled, and unknowing?
- What supports you in tolerating these experiences? What one or two resources can you bring with you and get to know through ongoing practice?
- How might you begin walking in an uncomfortable direction in your own life with gentleness and care?

Retreat Participant Poems

Prayer as I Enter the Dark

Patti Joy Posan

I am humbled
An invitation to welcome darkness
knocks at my door
Divine Mother
be with me as I greet the darkness
May the cloak of peace and hope
wrap around me
May I
listen to the voices

see the beauty in knowing
hear with an open heart
feel the caress of darkness
touch and not be afraid
And emerge above the murky waters
and bloom with the beauty of a lotus
And as the rhythm of joy moves through my body
may I, as a butterfly, know lightness of being
And be renewed.
Amen

Everything Matters

William Dinglas

Time is a companion,
That goes with us,
On the journey.
To remind us to cherish,
Every moment.
Because it will never,
Come again.

What we leave behind,
Is not as important,
As how we have lived.

Because the only thing,
We take into heaven,
Is what we gave away,
Here on Earth.

Everything Matters in Life,
For what we do,
And what we fail to do.

2

SPIRITUAL BYPASSING AND SHADOW WORK

So don't be frightened, dear friend, if a sadness confronts you larger than any you have ever known, casting its shadow over all you do. You must think that something is happening within you and remember that life has not forgotten you; it holds you in its hand and will not let you fall. Why would you want to exclude from your life any uneasiness, any pain, any depression, since you don't know what work they are accomplishing within you?

–Rainer Maria Rilke,
Letters to a Young Poet

When we commit to a spiritual path and to practicing prayer and meditation regularly, a couple of things might happen. First, we might be drawn to spirituality in an effort to avoid difficult feelings we are experiencing. We might be tempted to think that focusing on hope, light, and love will help us to bypass the very real challenges of being human.

Second, we might be seduced into thinking that once we are on a spiritual path we shouldn't experience anything challenging in our lives anymore. We might start to believe that any grief or anger that does arise is somehow a sign we are deficient or not praying enough. We can develop a cognitive dissonance between who we imagine we "should" be as people of faith and prayer and what we experience as vulnerable human beings.

John Welwood, a Buddhist teacher and psychotherapist in the 1980s, described how becoming a "spiritual person" can sometimes be a way that we build up an inner defense against those parts of self we find too uncomfortable or shameful:

> Being a good spiritual practitioner can become what I
> call a compensatory identity that covers up and defends
> against an underlying deficient identity, where we feel
> badly about ourselves, not good enough, or basically
> lacking. Then, although we may be practicing diligently,
> our spiritual practice can be used in the service of deni-
> al and defense. And when spiritual practice is used to
> bypass our real-life human issues, it becomes compart-
> mentalized in a separate zone of our life and remains
> unintegrated with our overall functioning.[1]

The term *spiritual bypassing* was coined by Welwood to help explain what happens when we try to bypass our very real psychological and emotional issues and needs. We split ourselves between the spiritual and the human, and the spiritual becomes elevated at the expense of our humanity. Meditation can be a way to disconnect from feelings that make us uncomfortable. In this way, meditation can actually be counterproductive in those moments when strong feelings arise that need therapeutic and relational holding, rather than immersion into a solo practice.

Welwood observed in his community "a widespread tendency to use spiritual ideas and practices to sidestep or avoid facing unresolved emotional issues, psychological wounds, and unfinished developmen-tal tasks."[2] This habit can be found in all spiritual communities and churches and is a way of using spiritual ideals of hope, joy, and liber-ation to avoid the messiness of human living.

Spiritual bypassing rests on an assumption that if we are spiritual people who regularly pray and meditate, we should somehow be above the challenges our humanity brings each day. Sometimes people feel shame when they are on a spiritual path and are struggling with doubt and despair. They've been told to readjust their thoughts to focus on "higher" and "more positive" emotions and ways of being. This doesn't honor darkness as a pathway to deeper wisdom and compassion.

We live in a culture that praises perpetual optimism and wants us to avoid lingering in feelings of grief, anger, and other emotions that have been labeled "negative." There is a collective disposition to turn away from what feels painful in favor of focusing on awakening and illumination. Welwood also writes, "When we are spiritually bypassing, we often use the goal of awakening or liberation to rationalize what I call premature transcendence: trying to rise above the raw and messy side of our humanness before we have fully faced and made peace with it."[3] If we avoid moving through our grief, if we suppress our anger, we will experience depression or project our unsettling feelings onto other people.

When we are spiritually bypassing, we suppress our shadow sides and try to pretend everything is okay when it isn't. We try to minimize "negative" feelings and avoid dealing with our emotional pain in any depth. We may end up feeling deep shame about not having the "right" thoughts.

When we blame ourselves for the suffering we experience, we become internally divided. This is a key problem in spiritual bypassing. We lose all compassion toward our tender selves. Shame, blame, and "negativity" move us further away from our deep heart's core, which rests in the divine embrace. Popular bypassing language includes the often-used phrase "everything happens for a reason," or saying something was "meant to be" because "everything is unfolding just as it needs to," or blaming people for their own misfortune—whether illness or loss of income or relationship—because they weren't thinking the right thoughts. This became even more pronounced several years ago with the release of the book *The Secret*, which presented the "Law of Attraction" and was all about how to adjust your thoughts so you can attain whatever it is you desire and avoid those things you don't. It is a terribly uncompassionate way of relating with others in our lives, to essentially blame them for any dark feelings they may be experiencing.

When I hear someone saying these kinds of things, what I hear is that the person is unwilling to sit in the darkness, the pain, and the unbearable ache life can bring. What I hear is a kind of spiritual fundamentalism that thinks it has suffering figured out. Bypassing is an effort to rush someone to meaning making without taking the vital pilgrimage of descent first.

In his book *The Solace of Fierce Landscapes*, theologian Belden Lane asks the potent question, "What can be said of God that may be spoken without shame in the presence of those who are dying?"[4] When I hear some of these trite, dismissive phrases aimed at undermining our experiences of loss, I think, *Could you say this to someone whose life has been utterly devastated by loss?*

Ultimately, why terrible things happen, we do not know. Some of it we can attribute to human brokenness; other tragedies are out of our control. This does not change the fact that our call is to stay awake through the midwinter, to not numb ourselves when possible and run away from the dark journey. The journey itself may offer up grace in abundance and transformation beyond anything you could imagine, but this is not the reason it occurred. God does not dole out suffering in some kind of cosmic test for rewards we do not understand. The midwinter journey is a descent into mystery and a resistance to the desire to create neat explanations for all that is beyond our comprehension.

When we engage in spiritual bypassing, it also relieves us from any need to look at systemic factors and work for social justice to repair unjust systems. If we blame those who live in poverty for not having the right mindset or praying enough, we absolve ourselves of having to do the hard work of asking why poverty exists in the first place. If we blame a friend for their cancer diagnosis by telling them they brought it on themselves through anger or other kinds of thoughts, we deny the realities of genetic predispositions and toxins that are plentiful in the air we breathe and water we drink. We reject the reality that healthcare is not accessed equally by people due to their skin color or economic situation. While we have responsibility for our actions and choices in the world, we alone are not responsible for creating the reality we experience.

Public theologian Damon Garcia writes in his book *The God Who Riots* about Jesus healing people and forgiving their sins as an act of "undoing the psychological guilt" and harm perpetrated on them by others. Jesus freed them from always looking inward to their causes of suffering and allowed them to start looking outward at the culture that kept them marginalized. He freed them from those who would blame them for their illness. This is still so very prevalent in today's culture, and Jesus offers us a subversive way of looking at this. Garcia says that every occasion of forgiveness is a revelation, "a divine disclosure of God's perspective of the world. . . . Forgiveness releases us from the cycle of self-blame and shame that prevents us from noticing the ways we are abused and exploited by our society."[5] This is a powerful reclaiming of Jesus's message of healing on behalf of those who have been harmed by those who wish to blame people for their illness.

A similar kind of message is at work when we hear people tell someone that what they are experiencing is part of "God's plan" and to trust its work in them, as if we believed in a God who was willing to cause us great suffering to teach us some sort of lesson. I do believe that God is intimately at work supporting us with loving and healing presence through our struggles, through which we can glean wisdom, but this is very different than attributing the cause of our suffering to God.

I have grown deeply as a human being through my struggles, and the Spirit helps to birth new meaning out of them. This is a very personal exploration for each person. Not every experience will offer a gift; sometimes the suffering is so great that we only carry the trauma and wounds. To demand someone else find meaning in their suffering is oppressive.

We may think that we are exempt from these patterns of spiritual bypassing because we have picked up a book like this and are seeking how to embrace darkness in our lives, including difficult emotions and challenging life situations that plunge us into a state of unknowing. But many of these forms of spiritual bypassing are quite subtle, and we all engage in it to some degree, myself included.

Think of spiritual practices that advocate simply observing, in a dispassionate way, our inner life and feelings. This can develop into a form of numbness where we witness our feeling life on an intellectual level but never engage in the necessary work of really being present to the embodied experience of these feelings. Our inner witness is a vital part of our spiritual work, but it can be used to keep us distant from the difficult aspects of ourselves.

Another form this can take is to overfocus on coincidences as signs of what is "meant to be." For example, maybe we miss a meeting because of an accident that causes traffic, and we think it was "meant to be" or somehow God-directed; however, this makes pawns of those hurt in the accident and those whose lives may be seriously disrupted by the traffic. It is a form of egocentric thinking where we are at the center of all of life's events. Everything becomes all about our own personal needs.

This is in some ways relatively harmless, but it is a form of magical thinking that can expand to other areas of life. When someone in our life experiences a devastating loss, we may be tempted to tell them it is all part of their life's plan, which is a rejection of the compassion needed in the moment. Trying to make sense of something is often our natural inclination when we are thrust into unknowing, but we need to be really mindful not to assume, project, or interpret these kinds of experiences in any way for others.

By reading about these subtle forms of spiritual bypassing and reflecting on their patterns, we can hopefully become more mindful of when we do this. A first step is to release our spiritual practice from the necessity of it making us feel better or more secure. Prayer is about growing more intimate with the sacred and seeing that compassionate presence everywhere, including in places of grief and anguish.

Although we don't want to overassign meaning to every life event, I do very much believe in synchronicities, which are meaningful coincidences. There is a playful, childlike quality to seeing some events in our lives as a sign of a direction we need to take. Synchronicity usually has a feeling of more significance in the experience, which reveals to us the deep interconnection of all of life. It can be hard sometimes to know whether the synchronicity is meaningful or not. One question to reflect on is whether my interpretation of this event is focused entirely on myself and a desire for control, understanding, or avoidance of feeling something difficult or whether it leads me to greater awareness, love, and care for others.

Rachel Ricketts, in her powerful book *Do Better: Spiritual Activism for Fighting and Healing from White Supremacy*, argues that the person who is engaging in spiritual bypassing keeps their own comfort as a priority. Ultimately, spirituality is "a means for us to learn how to withstand our discomfort and unpack and address its origins; it is not intended as a mechanism for constantly feeling lighter or better, for working around or away from challenging emotions."[6] When we seek only "positive vibes," love and light, forgiveness, and unity, we are engaging in spiritual bypassing.

Ricketts goes on to write that when we call on the "Spirit to help you move through challenging emotions or as a means to help you dive deeper into yourself and the ways in which you can honor and accept wrongdoings, repair harm caused, and expand into a higher, more aligned version of yourself,"[7] this is the path of true spirituality.

As we move further into a practice of letting go of our own spiritual bypassing tendencies, it means we must turn toward all the aspects of ourselves we have abandoned and disowned, welcoming them in with love. This is ultimately an act of letting our heart break and expand to include more compassion for all beings and their suffering.

In her book *Eyes Wide Open*, psychotherapist Mariana Caplan writes that in learning to feel life at deeper and deeper levels, we may experience something akin to a breakdown:

> Breakdown offers the possibility of allowing false structures to be disassembled so deeper discernment and clarity can emerge, particularly if we have a context of spiritual teachings, practice, and community to support us in mining the spiritual possibilities of breakdown. During such times in our lives, a doorway opens that may not stay open for long, and whether the crisis is respected and worked with from a context of spiritual transformation or it is seen as a pathology that must be

suppressed, hidden, and rejected will often determine
whether it is an ordinary crisis or a healing one that
presents a doorway to greater discernment.[8]

We so often demonize or resist these times of breaking down old struc-
tures, when there might be a door opening within us to move into a
deeper way of being. Having spiritual and emotional support is key in
helping us discern how to move forward in ways that reverence our
unfolding experience.

Deconstruction is an essential part of our spiritual journeys. Each
time we encounter something that challenges our previously held
beliefs, we are called into a time of deconstructing, of pulling apart
the old formulas that no longer hold. For example, we may believe
that God works in certain ways, and then when a great loss upends us,
we have to reconsider our whole understanding of the divine and how
this presence works in our lives and in the world. We might begin to
question whether prayer really works and what it is we are doing when
we pray, finding our way into new forms that meet us in this changed
reality. Illness can make us feel profoundly vulnerable and, especially
when we are diagnosed with something chronic, we may need to rethink
our work or family lives. This can be a very threatening and uneasy time
because we have moved away from the old certainties and stepped into
a space of unknowing. But it is necessary to come to a deeper and more
mature spiritual life.

This act of descent is a potent form of resistance to a culture that
wants us to always ascend, always produce more, always achieve more,
always be busy, and always be positive. It is a descent not just into the
painful feelings we have tried to reject but into the body as well, which
is where feelings flow through us. When we are cut off from our bodies, we have little access to the true experience of what we are feeling.
We will never truly grow as compassionate human beings without this
hard work. The more intimate we can become with feelings of rejection,
shame, sadness, and others, the more we can accept these feelings in

others and the less likely we will be to try and shut down someone else's expression and exploration of their darker emotions.

We begin by naming the pain and acknowledging it. Sometimes we will turn toward numbing, which can have its own intelligence. If you notice yourself turning away from emotional pain, try being curious about the numbing and turning away, being present to it, and seeing what resource can be with you in those moments.

We try to stay grounded as much as possible so we don't lose ourselves, and breathing helps enormously in creating space around the feeling. Start from a place of safety and connection to your body and your inner sanctuary, which we explored in the meditation in chapter 1. Then we can turn ourselves toward it and enter into it to have an experience of that which we have been avoiding.

Ultimately, if we are to sit with those who have experienced unbearable loss, we must face our own. When we have glib answers to why people suffer, we contribute to their suffering through our lack of compassion. Artist and theologian Makoto Fujimura writes, "If we desire to be there with those whose incalculable losses outweigh any sentiments of hope, with those who are too ill to have a future, with those facing the darkness of depression, we need to know how that feels before we can endeavor to be present in suffering. We need to learn to lament and weep deeply for the reality all around us."[9] Our capacity to be agents of compassion and healing is dependent on our willingness to be with challenges and not explain them away.

Emotions

Emotions are neither negative nor positive. If we spend a lot of energy trying to suppress any feelings of grief or anger we might have because we think this is an unspiritual way to be, we are bypassing. Feelings come as important messengers. Welwood describes them as "a form of intelligence. It's the body's direct, holistic, intuitive way of knowing and responding, which is highly attuned and intelligent."[10] We can learn ways to welcome in these experiences and receive what they are trying to teach us without acting them out in harmful ways. Sometimes this requires the help of a skilled spiritual director or therapist to open ourselves to the woundedness of our despair and doubt. We can only heal when we allow ourselves to feel the fullness of what is arising within us in slow, measured doses, so as not to overwhelm our nervous system. Resourcing ourselves is what allows for this titration, or slow doses, of experience.

When we reject intimacy with the difficult feeling states we all experience as part of being human, our lives become superficial, resting at the surface and always struggling to maintain an optimistic persona. Our spiritual lives never move beyond what feels easy or good. Unresolved grief is an enormous issue in Western culture where people are encouraged to "get over it and move on" without giving adequate attention to the profound pain and loss they may be experiencing.

When talking about the hatred a person might feel toward someone who has done them harm, we must be able to express this in safe ways without doing further harm to themselves or others. When we force forgiveness, the wounds beneath go unhealed. Tracey Michae'l Lewis-Giggetts writes about this powerfully in her book *Then They Came for Mine: Healing from the Trauma of Racial Violence*. She shares that her cousin Vickie Lee Jones went to her local Kroger supermarket and was shot dead in the parking lot because she was Black. Out of this horrific tragedy, she calls for replacing "our reconciliation efforts with actual spiritual healing."[11] She asks some powerful questions:

> Are you ready to be well? What if wellness lives on the other side of pain and grief? What if wellness looks like sitting in the discomfort of what privilege and violence have wrought on your fellow man? What if resilience isn't about pushing aside your trauma or the trauma you and your ancestors have caused but is more about sitting still enough to observe it—not maneuvering around it but moving through it? What would happen if Black folks released the need to show white folks that they can't hurt us, that they can't beat us? What if white folks

released the need to pander and placate when plain old reckoning would do?[12]

It is only when we are able to feel all of our emotions in safe, resourced, and contained ways that we become fully alive. Our capacity for sorrow is in proportion to our capacity for joy. The longer I have done shadow work and descended into my inner depths to welcome the difficult parts of my being, the more I experience joy in my daily life. It is not an immediate result but a way of being that welcomes life's fullness and embraces the paradox of beauty and terror both present in the world. We become afraid that feeling the challenging feelings will make our lives fall apart. However, it is the very resistance to feeling that causes most of our suffering. When we allow emotions like shame, doubt, and anger to move freely within, we gain more access to states like love, joy, wonder, and awe as well.

The poet Rilke saw emotions as bringing something new to birth in us: "Everything is gestation and then birthing. To let each impression and each embryo of a feeling come to completion, entirely in itself, in the dark, in the unsayable, the unconscious, beyond the reach of one's own understanding, and with deep humility and patience to wait for the hour when a new clarity is born: this alone is what it means to live as an artist."[13] When we reject our emotions, keep them at a distance, we are denying the birth of something new in our lives.

In her book *Healing through the Dark Emotions*, psychologist Miriam Greenspan tells us that none of the emotions are actually "dark."[14] We just have not learned skilled ways of coping with those feelings that overwhelm us or strike fear in us. Our emotions come with a gift to wake us up, to reveal something we need, or to inspire our action.

The Guest House

There is a powerful and well-known poem by the twelfth-century Sufi mystic Rumi that speaks to our work with our emotions. I invite you to do a quick online search for Rumi and "The Guest House" and read it through twice slowly. The poem is about radical hospitality to all the emotions that arrive at our inner door. Rumi invites us to welcome them in as all of them arrive "as a guide from beyond."[15]

Over time, as I lived into the poem's imagery, I began to discover a connection to the Benedictine concept of hospitality that plays a central role in my spiritual life and practice. St. Benedict wrote in his Rule: "Let all guests who arrive be received like Christ, for He is going to say, 'I came as a guest, and you received Me' (Matt. 25:35)."[16] The core of his idea was that everyone who comes to the door of the monastery, and by extension the door to our lives—the poor, the traveler, the curious, and those of a different religion, social class, or education—should be welcomed in, not just as a treasured guest, but as a window onto the sacred presence. For Benedict, our encounters with the stranger, the unknown, the unexpected, and the foreign elements that spark our fear are precisely the places where we are most likely to encounter God.

I began to see how we could apply this kind of hospitality to our inner selves, to all of the elements about us that we fear and reject—the painful and dark feelings, our shadow side, and the things we do and long for that we don't want anyone to know about. I began to see this as a kind of radical hospitality of the soul. The word *radical* comes from the Latin word *radix* meaning "root." Radical hospitality might be seen as hospitality that proceeds from the very core or root of who we are, an invitation to extend a welcome to the stranger that dwells inside of us. We are made up of multiple inner characters and voices, and some of them get invited to our inner table, while others are standing out in the rain waiting to be let in to feast and share their wisdom with us.

Rumi's poem commands us to make space for the whole range of guests who might arrive—the feelings we experience that we push back, resist, and numb ourselves to—which might come bearing gifts. What if we are the space around our feelings and through which they pass? This space is very much like the inner witness we cultivate through meditation. There is a quality of nongrasping, of not holding on to anything too tightly, of making room for everything to have its voice.

Theologian Gregory Mayers writes in his book *Listen to the Desert* that we learn early in life that shame is a barrier to what we think is unacceptable about us:

> But if we are to be whole, sooner or later we must sum-mon the courage to enter the pit of shame in our back-yard and deal with it, engage the demons, and pull up hidden things about our self buried there. These dis-carded and unknown fragments of our self will serve us and others well when they are cleansed of our shame, redeemed from the well of our own dark side, and seen for what they are. They too have a place in us. We are incomplete and fractured until we welcome and embrace them in friendship and love.[17]

Our wholeness is dependent on this extension of radical hospitality to ourselves.

What also strikes me about the Rumi poem is the fact that it was written eight hundred years ago. The psalms of lament were written thousands of years ago. Grief and suffering are ancient. As human beings, we have struggled with these difficult emotions for generations upon generations. When I remember this, it somehow places my grief in a bigger context. I am no longer alone in feeling this pain.

When the difficult feelings arrive, I breathe deeply and make space so I can listen to what messages they have to offer me rather than resist and leave them banging on the door. Some days this is easier than oth-ers; some days I still want to pile the furniture to prevent their entry. Sometimes it is appropriate to not engage, but when it is a life pattern and way of coping, this can be a challenge for developing resilience and being able to thrive. But as Rumi said so wisely eight hundred years ago, I am invited to "treat each guest honorably"[18] as a guide much wiser than myself. In that act of hospitality, I walk in solidarity with those who are shrouded in pain. I will come to know how essential kindness is. I will discover moments of wonder.

Practicing Presence

Sometimes, as spiritual seekers, we can judge ourselves when we catch ourselves in the midst of judgment or doing something we think we "shouldn't" be doing because it isn't spiritual, whatever that may mean from our own perspective.

This journey of growing awareness and compassion toward ourselves is the journey of a lifetime. I sometimes get trapped in the "I should know better" thoughts because of my assumptions of how I *should* be responding in the world given my commitment to daily spiritual practice. When I am fully aware, I usually begin to laugh at myself, at my own hubris, for thinking I am somehow not human. This kind of humility is very healthy.

This is precisely the journey. I can also get caught up in thinking, "I should let this go" or "why am I wasting energy on this?" Both are judgments that don't honor the experience I am having. They are a form of abandoning myself. When I realize what is happening, I take a deep breath; I pause and check in with myself and my body. I try to let myself observe my mind's actions—watching the loop without getting caught back up in it again. I let myself feel what is coming up in me—anger, frustration, sadness. Before I judge whether these are appropriate or proportionate responses to the event, I try to summon as much compassion and kindness toward myself as I can. This *is* how I am feeling. What happens if I just meet myself tenderly? Often the feeling softens, the thoughts release. I may get caught up in them again later, but this is just another chance to practice. Sometimes they intensify and I begin to cry without knowing why, but I allow the tears.

Part of the journey is trusting myself to have this experience, to give it space, and to keep listening for what this is all about. I must rest into unknowing.

Shadow Work

All of this demonizing of the darkness is also connected to shadow work, which Carl Jung explores so deeply in his writing, although the core concepts of exploring and befriending our shadow parts originate in many Indigenous healing systems throughout time. The shadow is everything we reject in ourselves. As we grow older, the journey of integration is to bring the shadow to light, to go consciously into dark places and befriend what we find there. We have each suppressed parts of ourselves in service to whatever role we feel we "should" play in the world. As we face the things we most fear, we can experience a profound sense of liberation and start to live from our own needs, desires, and power.

Generally in the first half of our lives, our focus is on developing a particular persona or mask. We strongly identify with our role in the world, which is often our work. We strive to achieve and accomplish, to excel and get ahead. The more we neglect our shadow selves, the more they grow within us.

At midlife, the shadow self has often grown enough to begin expressing itself through experiences like depression, physical illness, acting in a way we quickly regret, or dreams that feel disturbing. We need to release these blocked energies hiding in our unconscious by working with a therapist or soul friend, by tending to our dream life, by welcoming in emotions we would normally resist, and by listening to our heart's deep desires. This is a process of stripping away everything that is false about our lives and how we have adjusted ourselves to society's expectations. The journey of spiritual maturity is to embrace the wholeness of who we really are and let go of our need to control the outcome of life.

By facing the shadow self and welcoming those rejected parts back in, we enlarge ourselves and our vision of what our life is about.

Our shadow selves are all those things we would deny about ourselves. Shadow work disrupts our sense of self because we begin to embrace the wholeness of who we are. Shadow work is essential to this vital task of dissolving our efforts at bypassing our difficult experiences. Working with our shadow self is precisely the act of welcoming in, listening to, and integrating the wisdom there for us from our disowned and rejected elements. These are the elements we try so hard to suppress and end up projecting onto other people, convincing ourselves that we don't have dark emotions to deal with. It is challenging work too because we are usually quite invested in the masks we wear and the faces we show to the world.

Jungian analyst James Hollis writes, "Shadow is composed of all *those aspects of ourselves that have a tendency to make us uncomfortable with ourselves.* The Shadow is not just what is unconscious, *it is what discomforts the sense of self we wish to have*"[19] (emphasis his). The shadow is what feels strange, foreign, threatening, unsettling, or disruptive to the persona we have created. The persona is the mask we wear to fit into our families, our workplaces, and the wider community.

If this sounds challenging, it is. If this sounds like the work of a lifetime, again, it is. But in its absence, we sacrifice a life of growing depth and spiritual maturity. By softening all that has been frozen within us, we open a great river of meaning and purpose to flow through us. It is helpful to do this work with the support of others because we can be so skilled at blinding ourselves to our own shadows. Working with a therapist or soul friend can also help us from getting lost in our feelings while still working closely with them and feeling the rawness of them. Our shadow self is revealed when we pay attention to our bodies and our feelings, but also in dreams and in our projections on other people.

Carl Jung said that the central work of midlife and beyond is illuminating the shadow parts of ourselves and bringing them back into loving conversation with the rest of our inner parts under the loving and compassionate witness of the Self, which is the aspect of ourselves that is rooted in the divine. The shadow self is aspects of ourselves we have rejected to fit in with our families and cultures. They are qualities that have become repressed when we hear messages that we are perhaps "too much" or "not good enough," or that don't match certain qualities that have gained us approval. Sometimes the shadow self is what Jung called the "golden shadow," which are those qualities we so admire in others but are unwilling to claim for ourselves. We often encounter the golden shadow through people we admire greatly and put on a pedestal. We might find ourselves in awe of someone while forgetting their very real human frailties and limitations. We project onto others those qualities we want to experience ourselves but have shut down to fit in.

Theologian Barbara Holmes writes, "The human task is threefold. First, the human spirit must connect to the Eternal. . . . Second, each person must explore the inner reality of his or her humanity, facing unmet potential and catastrophic failure. . . . Finally, each one of us must face the unlovable neighbor . . . and the shadow skulking in the recesses of our own hearts."[20] This is the task we each must commit to; otherwise, we project our shadow self onto others.

Midlife is a time when the shadow self starts to vie for attention. Shadow material may start showing itself in our dreams or in our interactions with others. Usually when we have a dream containing something that repulses us, or we have an encounter with someone where our response to them is out of proportion to the situation, we can generally count on the fact that our shadow self is being revealed to us.

Midlife is also a time when we might start to question the persona we have been holding on to for so much of our lives. We may be tired of holding up a particular mask we wear and start to recognize how much of our inner life it limits. Our shadow qualities often bring us feelings of embarrassment or shame, and making room for these feelings while bringing compassion to ourselves is essential to the journey of shadow work.

Mariana Caplan writes:

> All mystical journeys involve a descent. Without it, integration is impossible. We travel into the darkness to demystify it and free ourselves from our fear that if we face it, it will consume us. . . . The trek into the shadow world is a voyage of retrieval. We undertake this voyage to reclaim aspects of ourselves that we perceive as too painful to allow ourselves to feel, yet these repressed parts are repositories of our transformational potential.[21]

The journey of shadow work is vital and essential for claiming these lost parts of ourselves. Hidden within the shadow self are vitality and creativity when we embrace the wisdom offered to us there.

Caplan later goes on to say that when we welcome in these unwanted dimensions, there is an "alchemical process" that unfolds where these previously rejected aspects are transformed into gift: "heartbreak becomes longing, fear becomes awe, greed becomes a tool used to acquire knowledge and pursue transformation, anger becomes organic empowerment, lust becomes a passionate relationship to all of life, sorrow becomes empathic compassion."[22]

Ultimately, shadow work is always in the service of health and wholeness, of welcoming in more fully all the parts of ourselves. It is also the work of a lifetime. For Jung, the shadow self was a place of incredible life force and energy. The more we draw on these parts of ourselves in conscious ways, the more we might discover our creative lives and what brings us real fulfillment.

This journey is one that demands we come to terms with the vulnerability of being human. It requires humility to acknowledge all that we have tried to hide, reject, and bury.

Whatever the origin of our midwinter experiences, they are an invitation to do the painful work of letting go of what gets in the way of living our deepest call and embracing that which has been rejected within us.

In Geneen Roth's book *Women, Food, and God*, she describes both awareness and presence as essential:

> With awareness (the ability to know what you are feeling) and presence (the ability to inhabit a feeling while sensing that which is bigger than the feeling), it is possible to be with what you believe will destroy you without being destroyed. It is possible to be with big heaves of feelings like grief or terror. Little waves of feelings like crankiness or sadness.[23]

The part of ourselves that is bigger than the feeling is the inner witness. Often our fear of our feelings creates resistance and more fear than if we just softened into our experience.

She goes on to write that we are to meet our feelings with kindness: "Recurrent negative feelings—those that loop in the same cycles again and again without changing—are unmet knots of our past frozen in time for the precise reason that they were not met with kindness or acceptance."[24] The cycles we get stuck in are the stories we keep telling ourselves—as knots of the past that have become frozen because they haven't been met with kindness or love or welcoming. Our patterns of inner rejection do not eliminate the difficult feelings but only freeze them in our system, waiting to be met with love at a later time. Trauma therapist Peter Levine says that "trauma is not what happens to us, but what we hold inside in the absence of an empathetic witness."[25] It is never too late to bring hospitality to our inner world and offer ourselves the gift of this loving witness.

Often we need support with this journey. Finding a good therapist or spiritual director who can be present with us and can model the ability to stay attentive to our experience can be an enormous gift. Leticia Ochoa Adams writes in *Our Lady of Hot Messes* how going to therapy was the hardest thing she had to do.

> It is so much easier to read a book on the five ways to manifest your best life than to sit with a therapist and examine all the times you screwed up as a parent. It is easier to look at your star chart or a personality test and blame your failures as a parent on those things than it is to face how the fear of abandonment instilled in you as a kid makes you go from people pleasing to burning everything down in five minutes flat.[26]

These things may be easier, but ultimately they leave us empty if we use them to avoid engaging with difficult feelings and skate the surface of our lives, never encountering the Midwinter God available to us in the fertile darkness.

Scripture Reflection by John Valters Paintner

Nathan Confronts David

> The LORD sent Nathan to David. He came to him, and said to him,
> "There were two men in a certain city, the one rich and the other
> poor. The rich man had very many flocks and herds; but the poor
> man had nothing but one little ewe lamb, which he had bought.
> He brought it up, and it grew up with him and with his children; it
> used to eat of his meager fare, and drink from his cup, and lie in
> his bosom, and it was like a daughter to him. Now there came a
> traveler to the rich man, and he was loath to take one of his own
> flock or herd to prepare for the wayfarer who had come to him,
> but he took the poor man's lamb, and prepared that for the guest
> who had come to him." Then David's anger was greatly kindled
> against the man. He said to Nathan, "As the LORD lives, the man
> who has done this deserves to die; he shall restore the lamb
> fourfold, because he did this thing, and because he had no pity."
> Nathan said to David, "You are the man! Thus says the LORD, the
> God of Israel: I anointed you king over Israel, and I rescued you
> from the hand of Saul; I gave you your master's house, and your
> master's wives into your bosom, and gave you the house of Israel
> and of Judah; and if that had been too little, I would have added
> as much more." (2 Samuel 12:1–8)

From a very humble beginning, David is anointed king of Israel.
He leads the Israelites against their foes and establishes a united
kingdom and makes Jerusalem the capital and the permanent
location of the ark of the covenant. But David doesn't "live happily
ever after." There's more to his story.

There are actually two versions of David's story in the Hebrew
Scriptures: 2 Samuel and 1 Chronicles. The latter book, written
after the Babylonian Exile, offers a whitewashed version of David's
life as an example to live up to. The former book was written

during the Babylonian Exile as a cautionary tale of how Yahweh's many blessings can be squandered and lost. There is no better example of that fall from grace than in this passage in 2 Samuel when the prophet confronts the king.

This story begins in chapter 11 when King David sends his army to lay siege to the Ammonite city of Rabbah while he stays behind in the comforts of his new palace. While enjoying the view from his rooftop patio, David spots a very beautiful woman. He sends a servant to find out who she is. She's Bathsheba, the wife of Uriah the Hittite who is one of David's soldiers away fighting the Ammonites.

Regardless, King David sends for her and has sex with her. It is unclear from the text just how willing Bathsheba is in this affair. But what is clear is that she becomes pregnant. David immediately attempts to cover up his sin by recalling Uriah from the front lines, hoping he will stay with Bathsheba while he's back in Jerusalem and so he'll think he is the father. But Uriah repeatedly refuses to enjoy the comfort of his home and his wife when his fellow soldiers cannot because they are away fighting King David's war.

David doubles down on the plot to cover up his affair. He sends Uriah back to the front lines with orders to place Uriah at the front line and then have everyone else retreat. Uriah is killed in combat. David feigns outrage over the senseless death of Uriah. Bathsheba mourns the death of her husband but soon moves into the palace and becomes King David's wife. The conspiracy to cover up one sin by committing a worse sin seems to have worked.

This brings us to today's passage, where the prophet Nathan comes to the king with a case to be adjudicated. The case is about two neighbors. One is a rich man with large flocks and herds of animals. The other man is so poor that he has only one ewe lamb to his name. When the rich man has a guest come to stay with him, the rich man steals his poor neighbor's ewe lamb to serve to the guest. King David doesn't even wait for a question to be asked but immediately condemns the rich man's greed and selfishness. He declares that the ewe lamb should be repaid fourfold and that the rich man deserves to die. In doing so, King David condemns himself!

Nathan explains to the king that David is the rich man, Uriah was his poor neighbor, and Bathsheba is the ewe lamb. It's not a perfect analogy and it does equate the only woman in the story with powerless livestock. But it works. King David can no longer live in denial.

Just as it would've been better if David had not committed these sins, it would have been better if he had realized his fault without needing Nathan to trick him into condemning himself. However, to his credit, King David does repent. And he does it publicly. He could have tried to keep all this, including his admission of guilt, a secret. (That's what 1 Chronicles does.) But David goes so far as to write/commission Psalm 51 so that future generations would know of God's forgiveness.

David's atonement is sincere. And if anything, the acknowledgment of his wrongs and his attempts to make amends here in 2 Samuel is a better spiritual role model than the perfect version presented in 1 Chronicles. To be forgiven and then try to have everyone forget would only serve David's ego. Sharing the whole story serves everyone.

Most of us haven't committed anything close to the atrocious series of sins as King David did, but none of us is perfect. And I'm willing to bet that most of us have tried to hide some action(s) we were not proud of. Shadow work is necessary and life-giving. In facing those dark truths, we can be transformed. And in sharing that journey with others, we can help others.

What harsh realities about yourself have you had to face and overcome?

Meditation

Welcoming Prayer

The practice of Welcoming Prayer was originally developed by Contemplative Outreach's late master teacher Mary Mrozowski. It is based largely on the teaching and wisdom of Fr. Thomas Keating and an eighteenth-century work titled *Abandonment to Divine Providence* by Jean Pierre de Caussade. I will give you a brief overview of the practice and then suggest you move through the experience in your own time and pace.

There are three main movements to the process of the Welcoming Prayer: (1) focus and sink in; (2) welcome; and (3) let go. You might want to have some kind of comforting resource with you as you move through this meditation, whether a prayer shawl or blanket, some prayer beads, a stone of some kind, or other tool. Then allow a few moments to turn your attention inward.

Breathe and slow yourself down; connect with your body. Shift in any way that will create a little more openness and ease for you. Then let your breath drop your awareness into the sanctuary of the heart and meet that divine source of compassion within.

Invite compassion to fill you, to meet all of your own wounded, hurting places with gentleness, with love, and with care. Then ask that divine presence to be with you and to help create a circle of protection around you, creating a boundary as a way of containing your experience, bringing it close to you as well as keeping out any energy or spirit that might wish you harm. Rest for a moment in that sanctuary of the heart, feeling yourself deeply held.

Allow some time to move your focus and attention to your body. Breathe and connect with what you are experiencing. Notice both physical pain and emotions. Bring your full awareness to whatever the experience is without trying to change it. Notice how you experience this in your body. If you feel sad, how is that manifested in your body?

Don't try to change anything; simply stay present. Focusing doesn't mean psychoanalyzing. This is not about trying to discover why you feel the way you do or justifying your feelings. This first step is the key to the whole practice. By becoming physically aware of the energy of emotion as sensation in your body, you can stay in the present, welcoming it in, which is the second movement. When you feel connected to the feeling or experience, you begin to practice this inner hospitality and say very gently, "Welcome, anger" or "Welcome, pain."

The goal of this practice isn't to get rid of the experience you're having but to be fully present to yourself and this moment despite the experience. What often happens when we experience something we consider "negative" is we immediately resist the feeling. We may distract ourselves or try to figure out what is wrong. But these responses simply move us further away from an experience in this moment in time. It is also important to note that if the emotion feels overwhelming to your nervous system, you can either try titrating, which means accessing 5 or 10 percent of the emotional quality and slowly access it that way, or pull back entirely and connect with any resources you have to regulate yourself again. You can always return to this practice at another time.

By embracing the thing you once resisted or ran from, you are actually reducing its power to hurt you. Open yourself to hear the wisdom it might have to offer, to reveal what it is trying to say to you. When we bring ourselves fully present to our experience, a remarkable thing happens. We can find the courage and strength to stay with the moment. We surrender the desires of the small self to the capacity of the true or authentic self. The authentic self already has a connection to the divine and is able to be fully present to whatever is happening from a place of calm and compassion.

In this practice we stay present, welcoming the emotion in, but we don't identify with it. We see that this experience doesn't define the whole of who we are. We are not made up entirely of our grief just as we are not fully defined by joy.

This act of welcome isn't about condoning the situation that caused the physical or emotional pain. Surrender isn't about accepting illness or rejection or pain inflicted by another as somehow just the way life is. You are welcoming in the feelings the experience triggers for you and letting them have some space within. This surrender is an inner attitude rather than an outer practice. Sometimes the events of our lives demand our resistance; sometimes we are called to say no. But the feelings we experience need room within our inner guest house because, paradoxically, it is only by inviting them in that we are no longer controlled by them. Once you are in congruence with your inner experience, then you can discern freely how to respond to the outside world of experience. You choose from a place of centeredness and consciousness rather than reactivity.

The third step is letting go, but the temptation might be to move here too quickly. The real work of Welcoming Prayer is in those first two steps, staying with the experience and welcoming it in until the wall of resistance begins to come down on its own. When you feel this inner fighting of the experience dissolve, then you can begin to practice letting go. This is just for now because as human beings we will continue to encounter the difficult emotions. This is not a final, forever renunciation of your anger or fear; it's simply a way of gently waving farewell as the emotion starts to recede.

If you feel resistance to the letting go, don't pretend; simply accept where you are right now and bring some compassion to yourself. If you feel overwhelmed by your emotions at any time, bring yourself back to your breath and your heart and anything that brings you comfort.

To let go, you might say something simple like, "I let go of my anger and give it over to the Holy One."

When you practice this regularly, you might begin to notice throughout your day that there are moments when an inner experience arises that you want to resist. You can simply bring your compassionate awareness to this process and, instead of distracting yourself from the feeling, simply pray the word *welcome* and allow divine compassion to flow through you, offering the gift of transforming grace.

Welcoming Prayer helps us to cultivate our ability to live with the truth of this moment and to accept whatever is happening right now.

Take some time right now; begin with a few minutes. Focus on what you are experiencing without changing it. Once you name the feeling, welcome it in. Stay with it as long as you need to, seeing if you can simply accept this as the truth of your life in this moment. Then when you feel a bit of release around your resistance, practice letting go, not holding on to whatever this was, knowing that each moment brings its own grace and truth.

At the end of your prayer, deepen your breath in a way that works for your body. Very slowly and gently, bring your awareness back to the room. Allow a few minutes to reflect on your experience.

Creative Exploration

Expressive Arts Unfolding

A reminder to use whatever materials you have available and feel free to adapt this sequence as needed or desired.

You will want to have a journal and pen. I will also be suggesting a creative exploration with mosaics. You can do this in one of two ways.

The first is to have a base of some kind, such as a small wooden board or box. Then you'll need a porcelain or china plate (or other dishware) you are willing to break, along with a towel and eye protection. (Please do this carefully; mosaicists usually wear goggles when breaking the glass or china pieces in case splinters fly. You can also purchase precut glass or ceramic tiles at craft stores.) And finally, you will need some craft glue. You can also use grout to finish your piece, but there is something beautiful as well in the raw, unfinished nature of a mosaic without grout.

The second option is to do this with paper. Take some construction paper in different colors and tear up a few pieces into smaller fragments. Then use a glue stick to glue these pieces onto a plain piece of paper.

Centering

Begin with centering. Connect to your breath. Allow your breath to bring your awareness down to your heart (one to two minutes).

Plant the Seed with Some Questions

- When do I try to resist or deny what I am really feeling?
- Which emotions feel the most challenging?

Connect to Your Body

Find a piece of music and become present to your body's wisdom and longing. How does your body want to move today? Or would it feel more honoring of where you are to rest in stillness and move in your imagination? Move with the intention of releasing any kind of certainty or control. Follow what wants to emerge instead.

Mosaic Meditation

Working with mosaics is a chance to be present to the broken pieces of life in a loving, compassionate way and work to bring them into a relationship of wholeness once again.

As I mentioned above, you can do this with actual mosaic materials, such as a base, some broken pottery or glass tiles, and strong craft glue to bind the pieces to your base. It can be powerful and cathartic to take something you own—a dish or bowl—and smash it into pieces. I recommend doing this outdoors while wearing some kind of protective eye cover. Wrapping the plate in a towel before smashing it can prevent splinters from flying, too. Keep pets and children away as well. Gather those pieces carefully and put them in a bowl. Then let this be a creative meditation of listening to how those broken pieces want to be arranged in relationship to one another. Use the glue to adhere them to the base you have chosen to use.

The other option is to use pieces of construction paper in various colors. Take a few minutes to tear some pieces up into small fragments. Put these into a bowl and sit down in front of a piece of blank paper. This can be white or black or another color; the background color will show through in the spaces between the pieces you glue down. Then listen for how the colors want to be adhered to the surface and let something new emerge.

Writing Exploration: I Am . . .

After you have completed your visual art exploration, allow some time to write and process what you experienced and discovered.

Name some of the emotions you identified earlier that are challenging for you, and for each one write "I am" on the page, such as "I am anger" or "I am grief" (while also holding the awareness that these are not your identity). After this phrase, do some freewriting to explore speaking from the voice of this emotion. You are entering into the perspective of that feeling and imagining how it experiences the world and what it desires. What does it want to say?

Imagine seeing the world through the lens of anger as a character. What does the world feel, smell, taste, sound, and look like? Trusting that the emotions are here to help protect you or process something that is moving through you, ask what wisdom has it come to share with you.

Silence

When you complete this process, allow one to two minutes to rest into silence, letting go of all the words and images that have come. This time of integration allows your body and soul to integrate what has been stirred up in the process.

This is a holy pause. Release your need to figure things out and rest into the stillness.

Questions for Reflection

- What are the most common ways for you to engage in spiritual bypassing?
- What is the function of this bypassing pattern? What is it trying to give you or protect you from? How might understanding its intelligence help you to befriend it?
- What have been some things people have said to you in trying to move you past the difficult feelings?
- What did you notice and discover about beginning to allow your feelings to have their space to flow through you?
- What is the blessing you seek?

Retreat Participant Poems

Untitled

Betsy Retallack

resting on the ground of being with angel assists
into this pot of grief is the incarnation of sorrow
a blessed slaying of the soul, lifted up by companions of sorrow
hope is but a window below in dark clarity

into this pot of grief is the incarnation of sorrow
even though I am undone I will dance in the stillness
hope is but a window below in dark clarity
you can always look into this place, it is alive with calm

even though I am undone I will dance in the stillness
a blessed slaying of the soul, lifted up by companions of sorrow
you can always look into this place, it is alive with calm
resting on the ground of being with angel assists

Untitled

Kate Kennington Steer

inflicting blessing on the other with each wounding,
wrestling in the presence of pain until the hours before dawn,
rest now in shadow, lie fallow, drink in the silence,
be awake to my wildness which has stripped you bare,

wrestling in the presence of pain until the hours before dawn,
until you are emptiness, a hollow cave of heart,
be awake to my wildness which has stripped you bare,
become a witness to receiving your new name,

until you are emptiness, a hollow cave of heart,
rest now in shadow, lie fallow, drink in the silence,
become a witness to receiving your new name,
inflicting blessing on the other with each wounding.

3

GRIEF AS HOLY PATH

Sorrow is part of the Earth's great cycles, flowing into the night like cool air sinking down a river course. To feel sorrow is to float on the pulse of the earth, the surge from living to dying, from coming into being to ceasing to exist. Maybe this is why the Earth has the power over time to wash sorrow into a deeper pool, cold and shadowed. And maybe this is why, even though sorrow never disappears, it can make a deeper connection to the currents of life and so connect, somehow, to sources of wonder and solace.

–Kathleen Dean Moore,
Wild Comfort: The Solace of Nature

Grief is not something we go seeking. It finds us all too often. In the aftermath of a death, an illness, or a loss of a dream or relationship, grief reminds us of how much we have loved. It also reminds us of the preciousness of life. In this way, grief brings us into an intimate and sometimes agonizing connection with our own aliveness.

I have grieved many times in my life. My earliest memory is when my grandparents' dog, a beagle named Euri, had to be put to sleep when I was about seven. Sadly my grandmother told me in a very matter-of-fact way, not anticipating how much I loved that dog. I remember crying myself to sleep for many days after hearing the news.

Both of my parents have died, and the quality of grief for each was very different based on our relationship. I mourned my mother's death deeply for many years, struggling with depression and doubt and ill-ness. In 2022, my mother's sister Nancy died. She was a very dear aunt to me my whole life and cheered me on in the years after my mother was gone. Her death felt like the breath had been sucked out of me. Most recently, the husband of a very close friend of mine died from leukemia. He was only fifty-five and a vibrant man who, along with his wife, was at the center of the literary community in Galway City where I live. The grief over his loss has been very much communal.

Our culture doesn't offer much space for grieving. Too often, people are reluctant to share when they are still mourning weeks and months after a loss for fear of judgment by others, despite the exhaustion we most likely feel. Even our churches give us the message to cheer up with spiritual bypassing phrases like "they are in a better place now" or "God needed another angel." These words, while usually meant well, do not give a safe space for the person in mourning to express their sorrow freely.

Many religious traditions have set periods for mourning. When my mother died, a rabbi friend of mine told me in Jewish tradition nothing additional was expected from a person who had lost someone close for an entire year. This was such a gift to hear, and it helped me to shift my priorities. The grief does not go away after a year; we will travel with it in one form or another for the rest of our lives, especially over a dearly loved one. But honoring the space needed for this threshold time when we live into a new reality without the presence of another is vital.

In *Entering the Healing Ground: Grief, Ritual and the Soul of the World*, Francis Weller describes how in Scandinavian communities, the one who grieved spent time with the ashes. They entered a parallel world when, like in Jewish tradition, little was expected of them for that first year. Their only work was to mourn and be transformed by it. Those who made it through became the wise ones of their community.[1]

One of the things I love about Holy Week in the Christian tradition is that, while we know resurrection is the end of the story, we still have a day dedicated to Good Friday and to sitting with the suffering of Jesus and our own grief. We also have a day dedicated to Holy Saturday, that liminal space between the death and the rising when we are called to sit in the space of unknowing. In her book of prose and poems, *Winter Hours*, the poet Mary Oliver asks, "How shall there be redemption and resurrection unless there has been great sorrow? And isn't struggle and rising the real work of our lives?"[2] It is only when we come into full spiritual maturity that we can hold the truth of life's devastation and suffering alongside the tremendous beauty and wonder of life as well.

Grief demands our vulnerability. It asks our hearts to soften their stony exteriors and allow ourselves to be undone by loss. To really feel the impact of our love. Grief is the agreement we make when we open our hearts wide to another person or being, whether animal or tree or landscape. It reminds us for the rest of our lives how much we have been impacted by another.

Grief can have different movements. Sometimes we are in denial, disbelief and numbness arriving like an initial protective layer. Then, if given the space, feelings can emerge of sadness, grief, or shock. Sometimes then anger arises or a desire to blame someone for our loss and the raw and irrational need for someone to be accountable.

We don't always make space for the full spectrum of what grief brings and some of these feelings we might judge ourselves for. Holding compassion for any desires I might have to blame someone for the pain helps me to move toward softening. Grief is an ever-shifting landscape. Francis Weller describes five gates to grief. The first is acknowledging that everything we love, we will lose. This includes the people we love, as well as the functioning of our bodies when illness visits. The second is the place within us that has not known love due to shame and being banished to our shadows. The third is the sorrows of the world and the losses we encounter all around us. The fourth is how sometimes what we expected in life, we did not receive. This might be the community or family we longed for, or the purpose and calling in our lives. The fifth gate is ancestral grief and all those sorrows we carry in our bodies because of unresolved traumas in our blood ancestors.

Weller describes grief as

> subversive, undermining the quiet agreement to behave and be in control of our emotions. It is an act of protest that declares our refusal to live numb and small. There is something feral about grief, something essentially outside the ordained and sanctioned behaviors of our culture. Because of that, grief is necessary to the vitality

of the soul. Contrary to our fears, grief is suffused with
life-force.[3]

I love this image of grief as something that resists the dominant culture's demand that we keep our emotions under control at all times.
I love the sense that grief is undomesticated, wild, feral, and a vital
aspect of our soul's unfolding. We can try to suppress our grief; indeed,
many do for years and even a lifetime, but it will manifest in various
addictions, in depression, in anger, in loss of purpose.

My father was born in 1932 in Riga, Latvia. In 1944 the Russians
invaded, and he and his family had to flee to Vienna where his grandparents lived. He was never able to return to Riga again, and he never
once spoke to me of the trauma he experienced or the grief he felt.
Sadly, it led to a lifetime of addictions for him, trying to fill the gnawing
emptiness. I carry that ancestral grief in my body.

Grief work is holy work. To be with grief in this intimate and profound way requires a container. A container is a holding space that
feels safe enough to let our guard down. This might be with a therapist or soul friend who makes space for us to feel what we need to feel
and doesn't rush us onward. This might be on our own, by grounding
ourselves well to begin, staying connected to our breathing, and giving
ourselves the space we need each day to weep and stomp and rage,
whatever is arising within us. Or to stay quiet and close to ourselves.
From a somatic perspective, the art is to stay aware and present and
to keep resourcing as much as you can while expressing these strong
emotions.

Grief is an embodied experience. Dance and other kinds of free
movement create a container to help us process what we are feeling. It
can be the smallest of gestures to the grandest of movements. You can
dance with just a hand or a finger and have it be a powerful experience
or dance in a full-bodied way if that is within your capacity and ability.
A journal can be a safe holding space to process our emotions. In this
container we can experience the flow of our emotions, the great river

of grief being released and set free. It slowly brings us to a new way of seeing the world.

The darkness of grief can open us to the sacred present beneath the surface of life at all times, as Weller writes:

> Within this darkness we become porous to another world. Some crack or fissure appears in these times of sorrow, allowing us to touch other worlds, if only for a moment. . . . Whatever the experience, grief offers a revelation: In the midst of great loss, we find ourselves in the presence of the sacred.[4]

This is the journey toward spiritual maturity—to grow in our capacity to hold paradox and tension. We are thrust into terrible loss, and many times those experiences do reveal treasures we could not imagine in the wake of heartache.

Jungian analyst Clarissa Pinkola Estes describes this loving presence we encounter through the grief journey as the "golden field." She says, "At the center of a grief-stricken heart, there is ever a golden field—alive, flourishing with enough soul to feed all who come there. This inextinguishable heart of Love protects life-force essence there, even while all else stands in ruins."[5] As in Weller's quote above, through the cracks in our facades, the openings in our armor, we begin to touch another world that has always been here, a reality so much more expansive than we can imagine. We encounter the mystery of the divine in this holy darkness.

Dietrich Bonhoeffer was a Lutheran pastor and theologian during World War II. He began his work as a pacifist and eventually was involved in a plot to kill Hitler because he recognized that, for him, this was the only way to end the brutality. He writes very pointedly to his fellow pastors and church members that by doing nothing, they are culpable. He writes about the need to get our hands dirty, that living out our deepest convictions is a messy process.

While I was in graduate school, I became enamored with Bonhoeffer's work. He was imprisoned for the last part of his life before being

killed by the Nazis, and there is a book of his love letters to the woman
he adored. At the same time, Dorothy Day was across the ocean writing
about her commitment to peace and nonviolence, which she felt was
an absolute necessity. These were two people of great conviction and
passion who had come to very different conclusions. What I conclud-
ed from studying both their voices (recognizing that my insights are
limited to what they left in writing) is that they were both right. What
made sense to each of them given their context and circumstance was
different even though they were responding to the same reality.

Their convictions came from much wrestling and many long nights
in the midwinter. We cannot make absolute statements in these kinds
of situations. We must meet each moment as open-heartedly and
clear-eyed as possible and listen for what is called for in that moment.
Sometimes it means we will fall apart, and sometimes it means we will
summon our true selves and find our power emerging out of the devastation. It is not that one is better than the other; the response emerges
from what is happening.

In his *Letters and Papers from Prison*, Bonhoeffer wrote a letter
to his dear friend and to the woman he loved after being in prison for
nine months, knowing he would not be released anytime soon:

> Nothing can make up for the absence of someone whom
> we love, and it would be wrong to try to find a sub-
> stitute; we must simply hold out and see it through.
> That sounds very hard at first, but at the same time, it
> is a great consolation, for the gap, as long as it remains
> unfilled, preserves the bonds between us. It is nonsense
> to say that God fills the gap, but on the contrary [God]
> keeps it empty, and so helps us to keep alive our former
> communion with each other, even at the cost of pain.[6]

I am really touched by this image—the gap, the loss, is kept empty so
that we may remember what mattered to us so deeply. No church talk of
God's presence fills the absence. The Holy One abides with us, sustains
us in this wrenching loss, but does not fill the space of loss.

Each one of us carries grief, sorrow that has perhaps gone unexpressed or been stifled or numbed. Each of us has been touched by pain and suffering at some time. Each of us also carries the grief of our ancestors and the losses they experienced. Yet we live in a culture that tells us to move on, to get over it, or to shop or drink or eat our way through sorrow. Or to fill our moments with the chatter of entertainment so that we never have to face the silent desert of our hearts. It is the same kind of attitude that forces us to answer "fine" when others ask how we are, even if we really aren't. Even our churches often try to move us too quickly to a place of hope without fully experiencing the sorrow that pierces us.

The poet Mark Nepo observes, "Despite our fear of certain feelings, it is feeling each of them all the way through that lands us in the vibrant ache that underrides our being alive. To reach this vibrant place is often healing."[7] The heart is meant to be vulnerable, malleable, broken open by love. The ancient Hebrew prophets regularly preached about turning our hearts of stone into hearts of flesh. The psalmist sings in Psalm 42:3, "My tears have been my food day and night."

Our sorrow is so uncomfortable we want to transform it as quickly as we can into joy. We want to return to how we were before the ground beneath us opened up. But transformation comes only in our presence to what we are feeling and to express our emotions, to let the wild river flow freely. This is the gateway to transformation.

Theologian Belden Lane, in his beautiful book about desert wisdom and his accompaniment of his mother through the journey of dying, writes about the dance between grief and love, between loss and wonder:

> It is a deep mystery that love is born in the mind's (and body's) experience of emptiness and loss. The longing of the soul, made sharper by the painful absence of that which it loves—by its inability to close on what it desires—reaches through the dark night of the senses, as John of the Cross would express it, to offer freely in love what no human effort could buy.

> If God is to be loved as God loves, it will happen only
> in the dark corridors of emptiness. Only in devastating
> loss—beyond the security of language and identity, in
> despairing ever of obtaining the glory first sought—only
> then does a truth too wondrous to be grasped come
> rushing back out of the void. Love takes wing where
> calculation ends.[8]

The whole quote is powerful, but that last phrase especially. It is only
when we reach the limits of what our mind can control and plan for
that we are broken open to something much more vast and expansive.

Why do we work so hard to resist our tears? Jesus wept. We see him
in John's gospel shedding tears over the death of his friend Lazarus;
in Luke's gospel, we see him weeping over the whole city of Jerusalem
because of their indifference. He grieves over both personal relationship and social injustice.

What is the sorrow you carry with you today? Is it because of personal loss? A death, a job loss, a broken relationship, or an illness? Is it
because of the thousands of children who will die today due to prevent-
able hunger? Is it the ongoing racism that devastates communities or
the religious hostilities that divide nations? Is it the thousands of people
who have died as a result of the years of war? Is it the devastating loss
of creatures and ecosystems due to the climate crisis? Perhaps the grief
you carry is layered with many of these.

We resist feeling our pain because our society discourages it. Even
without the absence of permission to feel sorrow, how many of us have
the time and space it requires to adequately mourn our losses? Beyond
the brief sound bites we receive in the news each night, where are the
space and the resources we need to process our sorrow?

Making Room for Despair

The poet Denise Levertov described in her poem "The Love of Morning"
that even with the burden of all the horrors in the world, each morning
we still "wake to birdsong."[9]

I have come to recognize and honor a deep despair that resides in the shadow part of myself, the shadow being of course those things about ourselves we don't want to embrace. And yet the journey toward our own wholeness is precisely about naming our shadows, welcoming them into the inner rooms of our being, and listening for what they have to say to us.

Family systems and ancestry work is a significant part of my spiritual journey. My father was someone who let despair consume him; his whole life he ran from his own darkness. In addition to whatever pain he experienced within his own family, his youth was layered against the backdrop of World War II, and the trauma and despair of that experience is something he never spoke of to me. I have found that resisting the despair only magnifies the weight of it.

Sometimes I am reluctant to share this naming of my despair because I fear that others will try to step in to offer me hope as an antidote. I have an ambivalent relationship to the word *hope*—too often I think we use that term as a way of trying to circumvent the necessary process of facing our own dark emotions. We do violence to others by trying to move them to a place where we feel much more comfortable.

Mythologist Michael Meade makes a compelling case for despair in dark times:

> Yet despair, so often avoided by innocents and cynics alike, is not simply a blind alley or a dead end. The territory of despair becomes the deeper ground and darker earth from which our most enduring visions of life arise. Not simply the "light at the end of the tunnel," nor a sudden solution from the outside, but the light hidden inside the darkest hours of life. Any hope for this increasingly hopeless world might have to be found inside the currents of despair that accompany the endless news reports of cultural unraveling and environmental disaster.[10]

It is when we are able to stay with the tension of ideas that seem in opposition, or in the fertile darkness where the way out is not visible, that often a new way forward appears.

I am blessed with a spiritual director who does not ask me to cheer up or have hope. He asks me to walk right into the grief, to name the darkness and pain and suffering that weighs on me at times. He invites me to rest there and imagine the pain my father struggled with so that I might cultivate more compassion and forgiveness for him and see those places in myself.

I want to resist the despair, as many of us would. I sometimes spend a lot of energy doing precisely that. I don't want to leap into the dark abyss where I must come to terms with the fact that this next moment could be my last, that those I love deeply will one day be gone, that we have waged countless terrible wars whose trauma will ripple through generations to come, that we continue to wreak havoc on our planet and so much of the damage is simply irreversible.

When I contemplate the unimaginable horrors of the Holocaust and other forms of genocide, I come to the conclusion that there is simply no consolation for that devastation. For some despair, there simply is no tidy redemption offered in response; it simply is the horror that it is. Not that there weren't stories of tremendous courage and love that rose from the ashes of that event, but the millions of crushed and broken bodies cannot be changed.

And yet, when I give myself space to walk right into that place of feeling utterly undone, of naming the things that give me reason for despair, I feel the crushing weight of sorrow and sometimes something quite remarkable happens. Sometimes when I am truly able to release my resistance to the places of darkness, I am reminded of birdsong as Levertov writes. I come to treasure the simplest kindness; my heart begins to open in wonder at my own capacity for love.

These things do not outweigh the despair, as though the universe were some kind of cosmic scale. The despair and the beauty dwell together in the same space, not competing, but offering to us the full experience of soulfulness. Poetry and art help us to hold these in tension.

I have come to realize that the opposite of despair for me is not hope but precisely this experience of wonder. Wonder that there is anything at all, wonder that in the presence of great darkness there is also so much beauty, so much love.

As you read these words, I invite you to notice what stirs in you. Do you want to rush and reassure me that everything will indeed be alright? Do you want to say that the beauty of the world really does outweigh the darkness in some sort of ultimate battle?

Or can you rest here in this space with me, holding the profound paradox of the world as best as you can? Can you join me in making room within you for the full spectrum of the emotional landscape we each contain within ourselves, responding to the call to be fully present to this wondrous and despairing moment?

I share these reflections because I think hope can be a tricky thing. I know I have been wounded by those who want to offer it too soon before being with me in the darkness. I know in our presence with others it can be very seductive to offer "hope" and unconsciously rush the person toward light.

Choosing Each Moment

We can choose whether to meet ourselves with hospitality and kindness; we can choose to inhabit our feelings or to numb ourselves and let them become frozen inside of us. Even once we make a commitment to allow space for our emotions to flow, we will inevitably resist them at times as well.

Several years ago when I was in the midst of a period of despair in my life, after my mother's death, I went to see a performance of Shakespeare's *Hamlet*. When the line "to be or not to be" was uttered, I found myself halted before those words. I had heard this famous phrase dozens of times before but had never really contemplated its weight and meaning for myself. To *be* or *not* to be—*that* is the question. I suddenly realized that in the midst of my despair, I had a deep desire to *be*. It was tempting at times to think about *not being* in the heart of that profound ache. Sometimes meeting ourselves can feel so overwhelming that we might ask ourselves what the point is.

In these dark days we live in, we can never know whether what we are doing, the work we engage in, really makes a difference. But we must continue doing it when we are able nonetheless; the showing up to ourselves and to the world of grief around us makes a difference. There is a dance of presence and absence at work in us. Sometimes the absence and numbing are inevitable, there to protect us from something that feels unbearable, and even have their own wisdom. What is not inevitable is bringing awareness to this dynamic and process, witnessing our patterns, and holding compassion for them. Then we will slowly grow in our capacity for the hard work of being human and alive. Reflect for a moment on your own choices of being and not being. We all have ways we check out of life. Sometimes we need to disengage for a little while to refuel, but this is different than the patterns of denial we practice daily. How might you make a commitment to being more fully each day, even in the face of challenge? To choose to be present and to witness yourself with compassion when you feel absent?

The grief we carry is sometimes ours individually, sometimes it belongs to our community or society, and sometimes it is a global grief. And sometimes the grief we carry comes from generations before us, our ancestors who were wounded in their own ways through war and heartbreak. In her book *This Here Flesh*, Cole Arthur Riley writes, "I believe in a spiritual realm that is so enmeshed with the physical that it is imperceptible. I believe in the mysterious nearness of my ancestors, but I believe they are located at the site of my own blood and bone."[11]

We can call upon these ancestors, this Communion of Saints, to support us in our dark journeys. To remember that grief is ancient and that many before us have gleaned wisdom about how to navigate it, I find incredibly comforting at times. Another resource we have available to us is our loved ones beyond the veil. Consider calling on their support the next time you feel a wave of grief rising. Ask the wise and well ones to help hold it with you. We are descended from a lineage of people who each had to meet and then navigate their own losses, who had to dwell in the cave of grief and descend to the underworld. They have wisdom for us.

As persons making a spiritual commitment to a life of meaning, we are called upon to help make space for the grief of others again and again. Yet we can do this with real integrity only if we are making space for our own grief. We can be with the pain another person is carrying only if we have met that pain inside ourselves. Otherwise, we will rush to comfort and assure and offer hope before the hard journey is taken. What we most often need to offer is simply the loving and compassionate space where it is all welcome. When we cultivate our own inner witness, we offer that gift to those with whom we sit. They experience us as the witness in their lives, and slowly, they may discover their own.

Scripture Reflection by John Valters Paintner

The Death of Lazarus

When she had said this, she went back and called her sister Mary and told her privately, "The Teacher is here and is calling for you." And when she heard it, she got up quickly and went to him. Now Jesus had not yet come to the village but was still at the place where Martha had met him. The Jews who were with her in the house consoling her saw Mary get up quickly and go out. They followed her because they thought that she was going to the tomb to weep there. When Mary came where Jesus was and saw him, she knelt at his feet and said to him, "Lord, if you had been here, my brother would not have died." When Jesus saw her weeping and the Jews who came with her also weeping, he was greatly disturbed in spirit and deeply moved. He said, "Where have you laid him?" They said to him, "Lord, come and see." Jesus began to weep. So the Jews said, "See how he loved him!" (John 11:28-36)

In the two previous chapters, Jesus heals a blind man and is criticized by the Pharisees for doing so on the Sabbath. The ensuing controversy, whether Jesus is the long-awaited Messiah or an unholy demon, divides the community. Jesus tries to use the physical healing of the blind man as a metaphor for spiritual healing, but this just further divides people's opinion of Jesus.

It is in this context, having just been threatened with violence and run out of town, that Jesus learns some troubling news at the start of chapter 11. Lazarus, a dear friend (and brother of Mary and Martha) is gravely ill. Jesus tells his disciples that the illness will not end in death, and so he waits a couple of days before traveling to be with his friends. Some disciples are reluctant to go to Judea because of the threats from their fellow Jews. Jesus encourages them to not be afraid. But Jesus does tell them that Lazarus has died and so he will go to Judea. Thomas the Twin, who is worried that Jesus will be stoned to death if he travels through Judea to see Lazarus, suggests that all the disciples go with Jesus . . . even if it means their death.

The chapter ends with Jesus raising Lazarus from the dead. But not before he stops first to comfort Lazarus's family and friends. And even though Jesus says that this was all part of his plan so that people would come to believe that he is the Messiah, he is still moved by the sorrow of Lazarus's family and friends caused by his death.

The focus of the story, naturally, is on the great miracle of raising Lazarus from the dead. But there are a lot of other people and things happening in this story. Jesus is not alone. He has the apostles and some new disciples with him when he gets the news. There is a discussion of whether they should go to Lazarus. And despite the risks involved, Jesus and his disciples travel together to pay their respects to the family of Lazarus. When he arrives, Jesus is (mildly) chastised for not arriving soon enough to heal Lazarus. Jesus is saddened by both the death of his friend and the grief Lazarus's family and friends are feeling.

The grief that is expressed in this story is very genuine. There are multiple individuals who openly weep. But they do not cry alone. Lazarus's sisters are surrounded by fellow mourners, and Jesus himself weeps with (not just for) them.

Grief, particularly the loss of a loved one, can be devastating. It is deeply personal. It's often private. But it need not be solitary.

Meditation

A Grief Inventory

This is a meditation on the griefs you are carrying. There are likely some griefs that you immediately know, "Oh, yes, I already know what grief resides in me." But there's been so much that we've lost, so many subtle things as well as more overt things, that I think it's worth reflecting on the really tender places that we're holding both consciously and unconsciously.

Take a few deep breaths as you are able and slow yourself down. Keep bringing that awareness back to yourself.

Rest again into the sanctuary of the heart. We're trying to drop down out of the mind. The mind can be really helpful, but in our prayer life it often wants to control or direct things, wants to make plans, or wants to make something happen. When we drop into the heart, we are moving into the space more of receptivity, of awaiting, attending, attuning, and aligning with this divine movement within that moves in ways that we can't anticipate. So we open our hearts to this, to welcoming in whatever the gift might be that comes.

In this sanctuary of the heart, I invite you to call on the name of the divine source, however you choose to name it. Because it has many names and many dimensions, you might choose an aspect of the divine source that reflects for you that sacred holding of grief. It could be Jesus weeping over Jerusalem, or it could be Mary holding the dead and broken body of her adult son and the weeping she is releasing. It could be the God of the Psalms, of Psalm 56 where it says, "You have . . . put my tears in your bottle." When I was grieving my mother's loss,

I found it really comforting to think there was an enormous bottle out there somewhere holding all my tears. Or you might call on a saint or some spiritual guide, maybe St. Ignatius or one of the desert elders who really knew about the gift of tears. Ask them to be present with you and for their support, for them to help hold you in your grief.

Then I invite you to create a circle around you. You can do that by drawing a little circle in the air around you, which is an ancient Celtic prayer of honoring the divine presence in all the directions. It's a prayer asking for protection, asking that we be protected from any forces that wish us harm.

Consider calling, as well, on any ancestors who are well and wise and healed. Call on the wise and well presence of ancestors who have gone through their own sorrow and grief but who have also made that journey of mourning and lament and healing, and who can offer a loving, wise presence to you.

Check in with yourself and feel your connection to the earth beneath you. That can be another beautiful source of grounding and connection and being held.

I will invite you to reflect on some questions and categories of events that you might have experienced recently. Pay attention to when that sense of recognition and heart tenderness is evoked, when you feel a knowing about the particular grief you are carrying.

Are you experiencing illness yourself, or has a loved one? Is there grief over loss of ability, connection, or future possibilities? Maybe there's been loss of income or a sense of security related to finances or health.

Maybe there's been loss of relationships in other ways. Or any kind of other transition that you might have experienced in this last year.

Think about your communities and your families. Perhaps there have been places of division in those communities and families because of different responses to political events that are happening or interpersonal challenges.

Maybe there has been the death of a loved one or a real confrontation with your own mortality, a deeper knowing of how precious your days are. Or perhaps you have lost a job and income and are at a loss of where to turn now.

Are you feeling grief over the ways our governments have not responded compassionately and in support of those who are most vulnerable? Do you experience grief over the losses Earth must endure because of our abuse and neglect? What other griefs are arising?

I invite you to spend a few moments in the quiet to listen to your own bodily response, and name for yourself one, two or three, or more, of those things that you're grieving right now.

Then I invite you to make a commitment to yourself, a commitment to make space, preferably each day for at least a few minutes, for that grief. Create a little grief ritual.

When I've gone through acute periods of grief, I've had a regular daily practice of setting aside a certain window of time to really give myself over to and imagine the river of grief. I let it flow through me as much as I could. This helped me to cope on a daily basis with all of the other demands of life that, of course, keep going.

Each time you sit down or you come into this ritual, ask for that support by calling on those sacred presences to ground yourself in your body, feel that sense of support, and invoke the encircling prayer. If you feel overwhelmed, pull back and rest in that sanctuary of the heart and do what you need to take care of yourself. Consider bringing one or two resources with you into this practice, either physical objects or a touchstone in your body that you can sense and feel.

We are afraid sometimes to open ourselves up to the grief we feel because we think we're going to be overwhelmed and carried away by it. Of course that can happen, but the more we can allow ourselves these small spaces of allowing grief its fullness of expression, the more we allow healing to flow. You might look to the Psalms and pray some of the lament psalms; feeling connected to the ancient cry can be a really powerful way to know we don't hold this grief alone.

Take a few slow breaths, and feel yourself back in your body. Call on the Sacred Source to steady you. Allow a few moments to reflect and make a commitment for your grief ritual in the coming days.

Creative Exploration

Expressive Arts Unfolding

A reminder to use whatever materials you have available and feel free to adapt this sequence as needed or desired.

You will want to have a journal, a pen, plain paper, and some crayons, colored pencils, or markers available.

Centering

Begin with centering. Connect to your breath. Allow your breath to bring your awareness down to your heart (one to two minutes).

Read this poem by Barbara Crooker:

In Praise of Dying

after a poem by Sue Ellen Thompson

Barbara Crooker, from Gold[12]

For giving us these last six weeks
where we reversed, and I read to her,
a novel about Africa, where neither of us

has ever been. For letting that novel
remind her how much she loved donuts,
their greasy faces shining through brown

paper bags. For Dunkin' Donuts,
their many glazed varieties.
For the afternoons that weren't too hot,

weren't too humid, that let me push her
in the wheelchair to see the koi flashing in
and out of the water lilies. For letting me be

her legs. When the end came, for letting me
slip some soup into her parched mouth,
rub cream on her hands and feet,

place a sweater around her shoulders,
all bone now. Watch her breathe
in the night, like she watched me

when I was new. For letting her
go out as quietly as a candle
that has used up all its wax.

For letting me be there
for her last breath
that fluttered out like a moth.

Plant the Seed with Some Questions
- What are the places of grief within me? What are the losses that still ache in my heart?
- How might I create a space of hospitality for what wants to move through me?

Connect to Your Body
Find a piece of music and become present to your body's wisdom and longing. How does your body want to move today? Move with the intention of allowing grief to move through you.

Gush Art Drawing
Pick up colors that call to you and draw lines, shapes, and symbols in whatever way feels satisfying. Let yourself draw like a child, without concern for making great art. When your thinking mind enters, release it as much as possible and try to return to the present moment. Draw to your heart the opening question. See what wants to emerge in response.

Writing Exploration: In Praise of . . .

Turn to your journal and write about what you are noticing. This isn't a time for analysis but a time for curiosity, inquiry, and discovery. What is emerging in movement and color? What feelings are arising? What memories or images feel important?

Return to Barbara Crooker's poem above and write the words "In Praise of . . ." at the top of your page. Then fill in the next word; perhaps it is *dying* or *grief,* maybe *loss* or *the ache of the heart.* See what words want to follow. Write without editing, letting the images flow. Creating a praise poem means you are not glossing over the pain but allowing pain and moments of grace to live side by side within you.

Silence

At the end, allow one to two minutes to rest into silence, letting go of all the words and images that have come. This is a time of integration to allow your body and soul to draw together what has been stirred up in the process.

Questions for Reflection

- Is our image of God big enough to imagine that God can embrace all of our pain?
- Can we trust that the God who cries out alongside us, whose cry is our own, will also transform us in that space of darkness?
- When you consider going to your places of grief, do you experience resistance?
- Or do you allow yourself to enter in open-hearted?
- What do you discover?

Retreat Participant Poems

In Praise of Knowing

Cynthia Gallo Callan

Snow gently falls now like frozen tears,
filling my eyes,

tightening my heart.
There is a darkness here.

"What do I know?" I ask myself.

Like forty years in the desert,
or forty days,
so do the past forty years,
find me lamenting,
gasping for breath
at my heart center.

"What have I learned?" I ask myself.

This grief will forever
walk alongside me.
Remind me
what might have been.
Self-blame will come,
then it will go.

"What could I have done?" I ask myself.

Interconnections of my whole spirit
rationalizes with despair.
Mind acknowledging
the need for acceptance.
Heart beats with grief,
yet also with unconditional love.

"Why is love so painful?" I ask myself.

The soul, however,
roots itself in guilt,
and shame,

embedded by childhood
beliefs and
theology of sinfulness.

"Why do I hold on to this theology?" I ask myself.

The mind knows
healing is a process,
tears must flow,
until,
like the melting ice and snow,
revealing a new resurrection,

Crocus shoot up through the earth
with hope, joy and rebirth,
releasing the grief,
bringing praise of knowing
that it will.

In Praise of Being Hated

Jan Spragge

For ruthlessly throwing me down wells of detest and cruelty
For throwing me against walls with brutality
your righteous lies
your cowardice
your lemming-like franticness
For tying my hands to the chair
so that I must look at who
what
how
I am
And for discovering

seeing
knowing
fully and easily
what I squarely look at in the mirror
is exactly what I wanted
I love what I see
more fully than I ever knew before
Your hating has set me free

4

THE APOPHATIC PATH
OR WAY OF UNKNOWING

To get to an unknown land by unknown roads, a traveler cannot allow himself to be guided by his old experience. He has to doubt himself and seek the guidance of others. There is no way he can reach new territory and know it truly unless he abandons familiar roads.

–St. John of the Cross,
The Dark Night of the Soul

In this chapter we will explore the apophatic path in Christian tradition. *Apophasis* is a Greek term that means *to deny* and is also called the *via negativa*—the way of negation. In apophatic spirituality, all descriptions of God happen through saying what God is not, as in the belief that with our limited human perspective we can never describe the full glory of God. The complementary path is *kataphatic*, or the way of images.

There are several great Christian mystics who have developed this form of spirituality. We will begin with the classic text by St. John of the Cross titled *The Dark Night of the Soul*. This is just an introduction to a text of great depth that can be explored more fully through many fine commentaries, including some of the authors I quote in this chapter.

John of the Cross lived in sixteenth-century Spain during a time of much religious persecution. He was imprisoned and tortured for many months, during which time many of his great poems were composed with insights into the dark night journey.

For John of the Cross, the spiritual life is not about getting closer to God. Instead, it is a journey of *consciousness*. We *realize* union with God; we don't acquire it or receive it. It is something we already possess, but we need to let go of everything that keeps us from seeing this reality. The dark night journey is essentially about stripping away all of our false idols and securities so that we might come to a more profound realization of the love that already dwells within us.

Even though we are made with love and meant for love, we feel separate and behave so destructively because we are asleep to the truth and we do not realize who and what we are for. We also misplace our love; we become attached to things other than God.

We move through life and seek God in all kinds of religious images, feelings, and experiences. They are the objects of our attention rather than the Divine subject. We yearn for a glimpse of truth, but God is too intimate to be a thing or object. We see God reflected or represented but miss the essence of the Divine being. John of the Cross describes God as "no-thing" or *nada*. In all the good things of life, God is not identified with any one of them.

Psychiatrist Gerald May writes in his book *The Dark Night of the Soul:*

> No matter how hard we try, our senses cannot savor God's ultimate sweetness directly. We cannot see God with our eyes, face-to-face. Our minds cannot comprehend God's wisdom. We cannot will ourselves into God's perfect goodness. Even our most inventive imagination can come up with only symbols and representations that stand for the Reality we desire.[1]

We live much of our lives rooted in habits, and because they are often enacted without awareness, some of these become compulsions. We may work very hard because we get praise for it or because we feel driven to achieve certain things, but overwork can be a compulsion, a way of avoiding deeper feelings. Compulsions restrict our freedom; we act in certain ways not because we choose to but because we feel compelled by habit or the trajectory of our lives. We begin to cling to certain beliefs, patterns, and behaviors not because we love them but because we are afraid of losing them.

In different spiritual traditions this is called *attachment*, and much meditation practice is centered on freeing ourselves from these attachments in our lives to things, beliefs, goals, outcomes, and expectations. It is an act of letting go of control of what happens, especially in those areas of life where we do not determine it. We are attached to having people in our lives and acting in certain ways. We can feel attached to a certain kind of job or way of life. When we grow in freedom from controlling life, we can meet life as it is with compassion.

This kind of attachment in the spiritual life is different from attachment in the psychology of child development, whereby healthy, secure attachment between caregiver and child leads to healthy relational patterns in adults and is therefore a state to be cultivated. We want intimate and loving connections, or emotional attachments, throughout our lives; these help to provide us with a sense of safety and anchoring in the turbulent waves of life. We need people we can count on to be there to support us. And we are called to grow in the freedom that comes from releasing our need for life to happen in a certain way.

When John of the Cross wrote about the dark night experience, he wasn't using *dark* as a metaphor for something evil or sinister. In our religious traditions, we have often divided our experience into dark and light with the dark symbolizing what is bad or rejected and the light symbolizing what is good or what we strive for more of. In John of the Cross's way of thinking, this is a holy darkness through which God helps us to release attachments and idolatries.

This is not meant to imply that God somehow "gives" us our suffering to then free us. Instead, as human beings, we will experience suffering as part of our nature, and through grace we can encounter God's presence there with us, guiding us and helping to transform our suffering into something meaningful.

The hallmark of the dark night experience is its obscurity—we can't see clearly and we feel disoriented; we don't understand what is happening to us. According to John of the Cross, the night involves us relinquishing the attachments we hold so dear and takes us beneath our layers of denial into the inner landscape we try to avoid.

Gerald May describes how John believed that in matters of daily life, it is good to have light. However, on our sacred journey, there is a different priority:

> But in spiritual matters it is precisely when we *do* think we know where to go that we are most likely to stumble. Thus, John says, God darkens our awareness *in order to keep us safe*. When we cannot chart our own course, we become vulnerable to God's protection, and the darkness becomes a "guiding night," a "night more kindly than the dawn."[2]

Our deeply rooted defense systems and patterns of resistance have a profound intelligence that tries to keep us safe. These patterns will arise, but we can build consciousness around them, which brings more freedom in how we respond to life. We are aiming not for transcendence of our humanity but for compassionate awareness. To move toward the love we most deeply desire, we must be taken where we could not and would not go on our own. To keep us from sabotaging the journey, we must not know where we are going either.

Fr. Richard Rohr writes about the necessity of listening with humility: "All saying must be balanced by unsaying, and knowing must be humbled by unknowing. . . . All light must be informed by darkness, and all success by suffering. St. John of the Cross called this Luminous Darkness, St. Augustine, the Paschal Mystery."[3] In a culture that glorifies knowing and certainty, this can be challenging for us.

John of the Cross distinguishes the night of the senses and the night of the spirit, and also distinguishes the active and passive phases, all of which can be helpful nuances. Essentially, these are all phases of a purification process where we either relinquish our attachments or they feel stripped away (usually we experience both) and we move toward greater freedom. These can include our ideas about God and how the world works, our theological framework, and even a sense of God's presence so that we can experience it as a time of utter loss and abandonment. Yet all these things are stripped away to move us more deeply into an experience of the love that dwells within us and in the heart of all things.

In 2003 my mother died. She had been sixty-one and not in very good health, but by no means actively "dying" (other than the fact that we are all dying in one way or another from the moment we're born).

I sat in the ICU with her for five days while she lay unconscious. At first she was hooked up to the ventilator and various tubes, and was receiving dialysis because her kidneys were failing. She developed a staph infection in her blood. The doctor told me that if she ever did recover, she would never be the same. I am an only child and was very close to my mother. I made one of the most heartbreaking decisions I have ever had to make, which was to take her off of life support. It was solely my choice, and the responsibility of that weighed heavily on me.

After five long days in the ICU, she finally let go on a Sunday afternoon while my husband and I were with her. We had just gathered her friends a couple of hours before to say goodbye and sing her songs and tell her how beautiful she was. When the heart monitor stopped beeping, I felt such a deep ache inside of me. I was now an orphan. Such a funny term for an adult woman, but in that moment it felt deeply true.

The next couple of years were quite painful and long. I was in deep grief, exhausted, and dealing with migraines and other physical symptoms. The first year was hard, but I found the second year of grieving even more painful than the first because I had expected it to be better by then.

In chapter 1, I shared a bit about how this loss thrust me deep into winter. The other aspect of my loss was how all my certainties about who God was as a loving presence in the world vanished. I felt this large void, this longing for my mother, and this longing for God. I questioned over and over why we would be created to experience such loss, why people had to die.

There were many days I wasn't sure I believed in God at all. I had moments when I thought, *Perhaps we have been just left here to our own devices.* Disorientation descended; my previously secure frameworks for understanding how the world worked disintegrated.

It wasn't until later with the wise guidance of a spiritual mentor that I began to recognize the experience that I was undergoing—this stripping away of every shred of hope or certainty.

I emerged from this experience much less sure of anything, especially when it comes to who God is. I have trouble with the word *God* because it carries so much weight and specific meaning to different people. I cringe when I hear fundamentalists speak with such conviction about who God is and loves. My own dark night journey brought the gift of a deeper ease with Mystery and a focus on what feels most essential in my life, which is Love. I am still certain that however this great Ground of Being exists with us in the world, this is the Ground of Love. If I do not have love, I do not have anything.

Contemplative writer Jean-Yves LeLoup writes that Fyodor Dostoyevsky believed "the atheist is sometimes closer to God than the believer who knows nothing of God except the ideas and images he or she has been taught."[4] Our attempts at theological certainty only move us further away from the divine nature.

Although I still have much to be stripped away, I've let go of some of these certainties. I had to learn to stay with the deep discomfort of not knowing anymore. I had to be with the pain of doing the work I do without being certain how to even speak of the divine with people who came to me. I had to let go of my ego's need to be able to speak wisely or clearly. Once I released that, it became easier to be a presence for others. I didn't have to have the answers or a clear vision of God to simply be with another in their pain, to witness them through their journey.

Howard Thurman writes in *Meditations of the Heart* about the patience of unanswered prayer. He says, "Slowly it may dawn upon the spirit that there is a special ministry of unfulfillment. It may be that the persistent hunger is an Angel of Light, carrying out a particular assignment in life." He suggests that considering this possibility can facilitate us slowly relaxing our tension while we recenter our hunger for something toward a knowing that this hunger reveals something unique about ourselves. With this shift, he believes at some point a person may say, "I know that there is present in my life a quality that is only mine because the hunger is mine. Thus, at last, I come to the door and seek entrance where there is gathered the great community. I know the password: 'Teach me the patience of unanswered prayer.'"⁵

Depression may accompany the dark night, but not necessarily. They are distinct experiences. John of the Cross recognized that there was more than one kind of darkness we might experience. He counseled to turn away from *tinieblas*, a depression that can dismantle people without putting them back together again. Then there is *oscura*, which means *obscure* or *challenging to see*. *Oscura* is a healing kind of darkness that returns us to our wholeness. This is where working with a skilled companion can be very helpful in our own discernment of what is happening.

Sometimes the dark night journey is a joyful experience. We also may experience multiple dark nights in our lives; with each time, a new layer of attachment is stripped away and more certainties are ripped from our grip.

The dark night season I experienced following the death of my mother was extraordinarily painful, and depression was definitely a companion. More recently, I have been experiencing some ongoing health challenges that, while a struggle themselves, are also leading me to a time of initiation into a new season of life. Midlife often brings more stripping away of nonessentials, and this season is asking me to really focus on what is most life-giving and nourishing. There is joy in this for me. The dark night takes many forms and can include joy as well as challenge.

In her book *In My Grandmother's House*, Dr. Yolanda Pierce writes about the paradox of faith:

> My faith—any faith, really—is a paradox. We believe what we cannot see. We worship One who cannot be known. We trust that which is intangible. Our faith requires us, each day, to face uncertainties with little more than a teddy bear or purse to accompany us. Our faith requires a nakedness, vulnerability, and a stripping away of everything until we acknowledge the essence of

who we are: creatures who cannot see even two minutes
into our own future and who desperately need to know
we are loved.[6]

This profound vulnerability is why so many resist and pull back from
the undoing the dark night journey demands, an undoing that leads to
a deeper and richer experience of the divine but can demand endurance, patience, and trust we might not have. I dream of a day when
church communities will actively create rituals of helping to guide its
members with wise elders holding space for those undergoing the dark
night journey.

How do we navigate this journey? We stay committed to practice:
to showing up for ourselves and for life, being present to our experience and not shutting down, and having a mentor along the way who
can offer us an anchor. There is no way out, only through the heart.
Ultimately, we take the journey alone, but it is helpful to have a wise
guide who has gone through their own dark night to help us witness
what is happening.

Impasse and the Dark Night

Sometimes we come to a place in our lives when we reach the limits of
our rational thinking and can't see any way out of our circumstances.
This is often the experience of the dark night, where we reach what
theologian Constance FitzGerald calls *impasse*:

> By impasse, I mean that there is no way out of, no way
> around, no rational escape from, what imprisons one,
> no possibilities in the situation. In a true impasse, every
> normal manner of acting is brought to a standstill, and
> ironically, impasse is experienced not only in the prob-
> lem itself but also in any solution rationally attempted.
> Every logical solution remains unsatisfying, at the very
> least. . . . Any movement out, any next step, is cancelled,
> and the most dangerous temptation is to give up, to
> quit, to surrender to cynicism and despair, in the face

of the disappointment, disenchantment, hopelessness, and loss of meaning that encompass one.[7]

In a genuine experience of impasse, our usual ways of operating become frozen. Our left-brain, analytical approach to life, where we try to force solutions and reason things out, is ineffective. So the right brain becomes activated, bringing its gifts of intuition and creativity, bringing solutions outside of our perceived expectations. FitzGerald describes this as a "reverse pressure on the imagination," where the imagination is the only way forward.

It must be stressed, writes theologian Dorothee Soelle, that if the suffering of the impasse is not allowed expression, "there is a corresponding disappearance of passion for life and of the strength and intensity of its joys."[8] Finding ourselves in this state of impasse, we must find ways of expressing the deep pain and anguish we feel, or else we will be destroyed by it or made completely numb by apathy. Lament is a necessary stage in the creative resolution of terrible situations and suffering. This opens the new pathway through and ahead.

The experiences of mystics across time reassure us that the usual rational ways of proceeding are of no use, but when we allow ourselves to have the experience of impasse, when we move fully into it, and when we bring our hearts of grief, only then can transformation enter in. The dark night invites us to reach the impasse of the heart and stay in that place of unknowing, to make room for all the challenging ways we feel, until the creative moment arrives again.

Scripture Reflection by John Valters Paintner

Jesus Prays in Gethsemane

Then Jesus went with them to a place called Gethsemane; and he said to his disciples, "Sit here while I go over there and pray." He took with him Peter and the two sons of Zebedee and began to be grieved and agitated. Then he said to them, "I am deeply grieved, even to death; remain here, and stay awake with me."

> *And going a little farther, he threw himself on the ground and*
> *prayed, "My Father, if it is possible, let this cup pass from me; yet*
> *not what I want but what you want." Then he came to the disci-*
> *ples and found them sleeping; and he said to Peter, "So, could*
> *you not stay awake with me one hour?" (Matthew 26:36-41)*

Chapter 26 begins with Jesus predicting his death. And immediately afterward, the chief priests gathered to plan that very thing. In contrast to the actions of the religious leaders of the community, a woman brings a jar of oil to Jesus and anoints his feet with it. Some disciples complain about the waste of money, but Jesus praises the woman's actions. Unfortunately at about the same time, Judas was conspiring to betray Jesus for money.

Despite the plans set against him, Jesus arranges to share the Passover meal in Jerusalem with his disciples. During the meal, Jesus tells the Twelve that one of them will betray him. All, including Judas, deny that they would ever do such a thing. Next, Jesus took the bread and blessed it in its breaking and sharing. He did the same with the wine, which he blessed and shared.

After eating, Jesus and his disciples went to the Mount of Olives. On the way there, Jesus tells Peter that even he will abandon him in the hours to come. Peter strongly refutes this, as do the other disciples. But Jesus reiterates that his death is close at hand.

This brings us to the Garden of Gethsemane, where Jesus takes a few of the disciples aside and confides in them how troubled he is. He asks them to stay awake while he goes to pray alone. He does this several times, but each time he returns, the disciples have fallen asleep. This does not help Jesus's impassioned prayers. When he steps away to speak to God, he throws himself on the ground and asks, even begs, to be spared what is to come. Jesus knows what has been set in motion and what is going to happen. But he also knows it hasn't happened yet. There is still a possibility, no matter how slim, that his death just might be averted.

It's the uncertainty that I think would be the worst, at least for me—the not knowing for sure.

In 2010, when I was still living in the United States, my mother was nearing the end of her struggle with Alzheimer's. It was a difficult period for the family. Alzheimer's is a frightening disease to have and one that ultimately can be just as hard, if not harder, on the family or caregivers. My mother had been diagnosed years before. Her decline was slow, largely due to the advancements in medicine and the excellent care she received. But it was hard to see her slowly slip away. It was hard not knowing when her illness would eventually catch up to her. When the doctors were sure the end was near, it was still months of waiting for that phone call. Even when the call did come and we went to be with her, it was still many days of not knowing when the last day would be.

However, in the midst of all that, my sister and I went with our dad to visit the mortuary to make final arrangements for the funeral. We ended up planning Dad's funeral too. After making those decisions, though, I found a bit of peace. There weren't any questions yet, just waiting. There was a sense of closure, of acceptance, that was based on knowing everything that was about to happen. There was no more uncertainty.

I find living with uncertainty incredibly frustrating. But that is something all of us have to come to terms with.

The apostles, the people who knew Jesus the best, didn't seem to fully know him. The gospels don't seem to agree on how much Jesus of Nazareth understood about his divine nature, most likely because they did not know. Certainly, John's gospel seems to indicate that Jesus always knew he was the third person of the Trinity, but the other accounts aren't as clear. In this moment, does Jesus know what's about to happen to him? Does he know what it will achieve? Or is part of his grief in the garden not being able to fully grasp how God's plan is going to unfold?

> Some may think it's blasphemous to suggest that Jesus doubt-
> ed, even here. But I find it more inspiring to think that, maybe,
> even Jesus didn't fully know but still sacrificed himself.
> How do you respond to unknowing?

Meditation

Trusting the Seeds Planted

Take some deep breaths and slow yourself down. Begin to drop into
your body and attune to your heart. Let your breath be slow and deep
and steady. Feel your connection and support from the ground beneath
you, feel your breath as a support, and feel your body as a companion
on this journey. Our bodies are the vessels through which we can let
all of our emotions flow.

Drop your awareness from your mind, which we tend to retreat
into when we're processing things. Drop down into the heart, into the
sanctuary space, and again, feel your connection to that infinite source
of compassion, whatever name you give that reality the mystics tell
us is at the heart of everything. Feel yourself being held in the arms
of compassion. Ask the divine presence to help you create a circle of
protection around yourself. Become aware that it exists not only within
you but all around you in every direction, and ask for protection from
anything that would wish you harm. Call on any other guides or saints
or mystics or archangels, if you have any spiritual guides in that realm
you can ask for support and presence, or any wise and well ancestors.
Take a moment to feel this enormous network of spiritual support that
is available to you from the earth to your body, to the heavens, and to
the sacred that pulses through everything that is.

Then take a moment to become present to how you're feeling without needing to change anything. Honor exactly where you are, not
arguing with reality and not trying to change anything. Be present
to what your experience is in this moment and bring compassion to
yourself. Then check in with your heart. See if you can remember a
moment this week when you felt anger. Honor that anger or rage as

a part of yourself that can be a sign of something wrong or a force for seeking justice in the world. Bring some compassion and care to any parts of you that feel anger.

Then check in with yourself and any moments that you've experienced grief in these last few days, any losses that you're becoming more aware of, and any sorrow that has carved a space in you. Honor how grief is a reminder of your love for this world and bring compassion to that experience of grief; hold it with endless compassion.

Check in with yourself again and notice: has there been any moment these last few days when you felt fear? Fear helps to protect us from danger. Simply notice and honor whatever it was that made you feel frightened. Bring compassion to your fear.

Reflect on these last few days and notice when you had moments of joy. Notice what brought you pleasure and delight, and honor joy as a way we remember the beauty of the world. Joy helps us to remember what makes life worth living and can fuel us for all of the other things we need to do in this world. Bring compassion to your joy. Make room for that and look at it with love.

Take a moment to honor that there is room in you for all of these: for anger, for grief, for fear, for joy, and for whatever other emotions you might be feeling.

I invite you to imagine in your heart's eye that you are crossing a doorway. This threshold might be dark, uncertain, but on the other side of this door is a meadow. Step across the threshold onto the green expanse and take off your shoes. Let your feet feel the grass. The sun radiates. The ground is warm. You're invited to lie down in this field for a few moments to feel yourself bask in that gentle heat. While the meadow is covered with grasses, there are not yet flowers blooming. As you lie there on the meadow, close your eyes for a few moments and listen. Can you hear the seeds that rumble? In that space of emptiness, can you let yourself rest into that holding space? The meadow with all of its possibilities? Then I invite you to imagine all of those feelings that you were exploring before—anger and grief, fear and joy—that each of those is a handful of seeds you can scatter into the fields.

You don't have to know what will bloom from these seeds. Rise up and spread them around as an offering. Then listen to the rumbling beneath you and ask yourself how you might yield even more deeply into this place of unknowing. What are the patterns, the habits of reaching and doing that you can gently surrender? Take a moment to listen, to see what those inner responses are. Then take a few nice, slow breaths again. Gently connect to your body; let it awaken a bit, and very gradually return your awareness to the room that you're in. Allow a few moments for reflection on what you discovered.

Creative Exploration

Expressive Arts Unfolding

As a reminder, use whatever materials you have available and feel free to adapt this sequence as needed or desired.

You will want to have a journal, a pen, and some clay. Play-Doh or self-hardening clay is best.

Centering

Begin with centering. Connect to your breath by slowing down its rhythm of inhale and exhale. Allow your breath to bring your awareness down to your heart (one to two minutes).

Read this poem by Dennis O'Driscoll.

What She Does Not Know Is

Dennis O'Driscoll

That she is a widow.
That these are the last untinged memories of her life.
That he is slumped in his seat at a lay-by.
That a policeman is trying to revive him.
That the knife and fork she has set are merely decorative.
That the steak beside the pan will be go to waste.
That he has lost his appetite.

That the house she is tidying is for sale.

That the holiday snap will be used for his memorial card.

That he will not be subjected to direct light again.

That she will spend all night brewing tears.

That it is not his car she will soon hear slowing down outside.[9]

Plant the Seed with Some Questions

- What are the things I do not know?
- How can I hold a place for mystery within me?

Connect to Your Body

Find a piece of music and become present to your body's wisdom and longing. How does your body want to move today? Move with the intention of releasing any kind of certainty or control. Follow what wants to emerge instead.

Clay Meditation

I invite you to work with a small piece of clay (either Play-Doh or self-hardening clay is perfect) as part of your prayer. If you do not have clay available, you can engage this meditation in your imagination. (You can also search online for a recipe to make your own Play-Doh with water, salt, and flour.)

Take some time to begin working with the clay and become familiar with its feel in your hands. Notice its texture and the way it both resists and yields to your touch.

Hold the questions above in your heart as you continue to play with the clay. Notice how it feels in your hand. Don't worry about making an image; just be present to the materials and to what is stirring inside of you. Let your hands guide this process.

Begin to notice if there are any shapes or images being formed in your hands. As you play with the clay, see if it wants to be formed into a particular shape. If it does not, honor that reality as well. As you continue to listen and be present, begin to notice if there are any images bubbling up inside you.

Writing Exploration: What I Do Not Know Is . . .

Turn to your journal and write about what you are noticing. This isn't a time for analysis but a time for curiosity, inquiry, and discovery. What is emerging? What feelings are arising? What memories or images feel important?

Return to Dennis O'Driscoll's poem above and write the words "What I Do Not Know . . ." You can also do this in second or third person: "What You Do Not Know," "What She/He Does Not Know," or "What They Do Not Know."

Then let the words come in response. What are the things whose meaning remains closed to you? You might write about one specific image as in the example poem, or it might be a litany of all the things you feel uncertain or unsure about in your life.

Silence

At the end, allow one to two minutes to rest into silence, letting go of all the words and images that have come. This is a time of integration, allowing your body and soul to integrate what has been stirred up in the process.

Questions for Reflection

As we end this week, pause and reflect on your own experience.

- Can you name your own dark night experiences?
- What were the attachments to things or ideas that were stripped away?
- What resources helped you through these seasons?
- What was the catalyst for you to experience the dawn (if that has come yet)?
- What does all this theological talk stir for you?
- How do you understand detachment or letting go?
- Has this been helpful for you in practice, or do you experience resistance to the idea?
- Where are you being called to say "I don't know" and enter into the grace of unknowing?

Retreat Participant Poems

Untitled

Carol Warren

What she doesn't know
is how far away the stars are.
"Light-years" explodes her head—
she peers at light shining eons ago.
She doesn't know what creatures
became extinct today—
animals, plants, birds, insects
removed forever from a state of possibility.
What she doesn't know
is if she'll ever dance with friends again
the way they used to
cavorting to the band, eating pizza.
She doesn't know if we can heal
the wounds, the scars that divide us.
What she doesn't know
is why some relationships last and others don't—
how she could've been other than who she is,
or if that would have made a difference.
She doesn't know how her life
might have been altered
if she has chosen This instead of That,
turned left instead of right—
or just stopped for a bit.
What she doesn't know
is how long they have
she and her true-blue dog.
Will she one day collect his toys
weeping over his empty bed?

Or will he live out his days
with her daughter,
puzzled that she does not come.

what i do not know (after Dennis O'Driscoll)

JoAnn Heiser

what i do not know is
everything
revealing as pencil marks this page

what i do not know
is very next moment

what i do not know ~
what to do
what is mine to be and bring
to these loved ones

what i do not know is
anything
what i do not know is
what is best for any other
their path their truth their soul calling

what i do not know is
filling this page
is open freeing wonder

what i do not know is making way for ~

may i honor and rest in what i do not know
aho

5

THE COMPASSIONATE, FIERCE, DARK FEMININE

Even in the midst of all our bandages and broken spirit-bones, (Mary) calls us to stop mis-thinking that we stand alone in our challenges, when in fact, she ever stands with us. We ought ever flee to her side, ever hide under her shoulder, ever shelter under her inviolate mantle, ever be guided by her wisdom so hard-won—for she too bore miracles, menacings, and sufferings in her life. She too lost everything precious to her soul in the darkened world of human fools, foibles, and frailties of spirit.

–Clarissa Pinkola Estes,
Untie the Strong Woman

A few years ago, I was watching my teaching partner Betsey Beckman perform one of her story dances based on the prodigal son, but in her version it is the prodigal daughter. As I watched her embody the "dutiful daughter" who stayed behind while her sister went out into the world, I felt this sudden sickening awareness. I knew I had always played the dutiful daughter in terms of my academic life; grades were the one place I could get approval from my father. But in that moment I could see how I had played this role in other ways as well.

Of my father's many addictions, sex was one of them, and when I entered puberty, he began sharing with me the details of his affairs and transgressions. He would tell me that I was the only one he could talk to and so placed me in an impossible situation. The message that was given to me over and over by my father was that women had to have sex with men to gain their approval. When I was fourteen years old, I began a relationship with a man several years older than me that continued for three years. I was so hungry for the approval of a man in my life to make up for my emotionally absent father, and I was being taken advantage of by someone old enough to know better.

As I experienced this story from a feminine perspective, I could suddenly see how this relationship that I had in my teenage years was one way I was pleasing my father, performing the role he expected. I was the dutiful daughter. I began to grieve this duty I had performed. I had long felt misplaced guilt and shame about this early sexual relationship. It took me many years to realize that a form of sexual abuse had occurred and there was trauma that needed healing.

I also began to grieve that no one in my life ever stepped in to say, "Christine, this is not appropriate. What this man is doing is unethical, unconscionable." There were adults in my life who knew what was happening. My mother objected once, but she was also drinking as a way of coping with my father's abuse and so didn't protect me. I found myself as an adult grieving that she stepped back so easily and let me carry on wounding myself like that for years.

I found myself deeply longing for the protection of a fierce mother presence, someone who would have shielded me from the harm of what was happening. I was longing for an encounter with the fierce, compassionate feminine.

I spent much of my twenties and thirties seeking to understand the ways I had been wounded by patriarchy and had cooperated by wounding myself in acquiescence to its power. My therapist invited me to explore how I had submitted myself to the "toxic gaze" and how I might begin to reclaim a different one. What happens when I see myself through the eyes of Love?

I traveled to Riga, Latvia, for the first time in 2008, the place where my father was born and spent the first few years of his life before his family had to flee because of the Russian occupation. I went to the church where he had been baptized, and when I asked for the translation of the name, I was told it was the church of Our Lady of Sorrows or the Sorrowful Mother. I felt tears rise. It made such perfect sense to me that my father, more than seventy-five years before, was dipped into the waters there in that space dedicated to Mary, who understands the well of grief. His life was spent running from the darkness he felt inside. Even though he rejected his grief and tried to hold it back with alcohol and other addictions, I knew in that moment standing there that Mary had been holding him all along. She carried the sorrows he could not face, waiting for him to one day soften and grow tender and turn toward them. It didn't happen in his lifetime, but I know he has found healing in death and Mary was there to hold him in that transition too. I felt such healing grace, such compassion and understanding.

I began to explore who this Mary was who knew the sorrows of my own heart. I have never been very much inclined toward the Rosary before but was intrigued by the meditations honoring the Seven Sorrows of Mary, which are traditionally named as the prophecy of Simeon (that a sword would pierce her heart), the flight into Egypt, the loss of Jesus in the Temple, meeting Jesus while carrying the cross, the Crucifixion, Mary receiving Jesus's body, and Mary placing his body in the tomb.

Mary is more than the Mother of God. She is one of the feminine archetypes who can help us to rediscover our own power and wholeness in the face of disorientation and disintegration. She points the way toward the fullness of our own becoming. No matter our gender, we each contain these aspects of the sacred masculine and feminine energies within us.

In making space for our sorrow, we can begin to free ourselves from this addiction, from this need to meet the demands of others. Mary abides with us in our moments of profound sorrow; she knows this dark loss herself deep in her bones. She points the way to our growing wholeness, to claim our wholeness apart from any other person. She is the comforter, the protector, and the one who reveals our own divine radiance back to ourselves.

The Black Madonna

In my book *Birthing the Holy*, I wrote about the Black Madonna and her many ways of appearing to us. These statues and paintings, which appear across Europe and beyond, are some of the oldest images of Mary we have. These images are enshrined in many pilgrimage churches and monasteries, some very remote. Some appear in the smallest of chapels or the grandest of cathedrals. They live in crypts and on top of pillars with millions of pilgrims seeking them out for healing and connection to Mary in her dark wisdom.

Christian feminist theology sees the Black Madonna as revealing aspects of the sacred feminine that are generally not represented in traditional images of Mary. These dark-skinned representations of Our Lady expand Mary's image beyond her usual depiction as a docile white woman. The Black Madonna roots Mary in the struggle of her Black and Brown sisters for justice. Even more than a connection through skin color, the Black Madonna reveals a dimension of the sacred feminine that is fiercer and able to stay present with us through our own times of darkness and suffering.

Mary in her Blackness offers us a fierce love in which she unequivocally claims that every person who experiences oppression should be nourished, cherished, and welcomed. She compels us to act for justice out of this witness of expansive love.

There are many theories as to the origin of the Black Madonna's dark skin. One is that these images illustrate a text from the Song of Songs that reads: "I am black but beautiful." The Song of Songs was a much-loved biblical text, especially in the early medieval period when many of these images of Mary were created. St. Bernard of Clairvaux wrote several commentaries on this book, comparing the soul to the bride within the text, and had a great devotion to Mary. He is known to have visited many shrines of the Black Madonna himself.[1]

In Sue Monk Kidd's novel *The Secret Life of Bees,* an image of the Black Madonna graces honey jars and becomes a character in the story. China Galland's memoir, *Longing for Darkness,* describes a pilgrimage in search of the same figure. The blackness of the images also has to do with symbolic meanings and connections to early goddesses. One of my favorite Black Madonnas is in the crypt at Chartres Cathedral; she is called Notre Dame Sous-Terre, or Our Lady of the Underworld.

Mary in her Black guise shows us the Madonna who makes the descent into darkness alongside us.

Theologian David Richo writes:

> Mary was presented to us as our prompt and perpetual help, and we love the consolations of her presence. Yet we seem unable to meet her as the terrifying mother who helps us grow through pain. Terrifying means frightening to the ego that cannot believe there is grace behind the terror. To invoke Mary for an exemption from the conditions of existence is to invoke her against herself. Initiatory pain is her necessary dark side. This is precisely how she helps us.[2]

Mary abides with us in the pain of life. She does not cause this suffering but sits with us and stays present to us as we endure it. The image of the women who sit at the foot of the cross, waiting in the midst of the terrible mystery of suffering and death, and face this evil in nonviolent ways is the image of sacred initiation of our egos being stripped of their securities into a much more mature and wiser way of being. When we pray to the Black Madonna in her fierce aspect, we pray for the strength to endure our own underworld journeys and not to avoid them.

Endurance means we are developing the capacity to make something substantial. The Great Mother teaches us endurance in the underground forest, the underworld of feminine knowing. It is a wide world that lives under the surface of this one, one infused with instinctive language and knowing.

Mary as Black Madonna is one of the feminine archetypes who can help us to rediscover our own power and wholeness in the face of disorientation and disintegration. She points the way toward the fullness of our own becoming.

In *God Is a Black Woman*, theologian Christena Cleveland writes, "In whitemalegod's hypermasculine world of reason, tradition, and certainty, the Sacred Black Feminine is entirely otherworldly, declaring Her truth not just through ideas but through magical and expansive experiences. Unlike whitemalegod, who is held hostage by logic, She also dwells in the feminine realm of intuition, possibility, and mysticism."[3] The Black Madonna stretches us beyond the rational and linear ways of thinking our culture so prizes and gives us access to the many other ways of knowing that are available to us when we welcome in the gifts of night and winter.

The Dark Goddess

In her book *Mysteries of the Dark Moon: The Healing Power of the Dark Goddess*, Demetra George suggests that the moon has always symbolized the constant fluctuation and change of our lives. We continuously experience these alternations of creation and destruction, growth and decay, birth and death, light and dark, and conscious and unconscious. It is the very wisdom our breath offers to us as well when we are paying attention to its full cycle. Unfortunately, in our society we have been taught to fear and resist the decreasing energies represented by the dark, by decay, death, and the unconscious. George goes on to say we have lost this essential wisdom offered to us.[4]

The dark goddess appears across time and traditions as the face of Kali in India, Hekate and Persephone in Greece, Lilith in the Near East, Ereshkigal in Sumeria, the Black Madonna, Medusa, Nyx, Isis, and many others. She symbolizes and embodies fierce and compassionate power. She encompasses the whole cycle of creation and destruction. Marion Woodman, in her book *Dancing in the Flames: The Dark Goddess in the Transformation of Consciousness*, writes, "The fact is the Goddess who gives life is the Goddess who takes life away. That fact allows for no sentimentality. She is both birth mother and death mother. In feminine thinking, we hold the paradox beyond the contradictions. She is the flux of life in which creation gives place to destruction, destruction in service to life gives place to creation."[5] The dark feminine is embodied in the cycles of life, death, and rebirth we continually experience. Mary embodies the birth mother and the death mother. Two of the depictions of her we see most commonly in art are the Nativity—holding the infant Jesus in her arms—and the pietà—holding her crucified son's body in her arms.

In ancient times, as people approached death, they would call upon the dark goddess for her infinite compassion. Those who were her devotees were often the funerary priestesses who cared for those dying, accompanying them through their last breath, preparing the bodies, presiding over the rituals, and supporting the grieving families.

George describes the fear of death as emerging from the left-brain perception that sees time as linear rather than cyclical. In linear time, the end is no longer connected to the beginning. The end becomes the conclusion of a person's life, rather than being seen as one phase of it. Death becomes the final terror and is avoided at any cost.

In a cyclical perspective on the world and creation, we begin to see that decay, disintegration, and death are only one moment on a wheel of movement. In nature death always leads to life. When I was in college, I once took an ecology class where I remember the moment of learning that the decay and compost of life into death is actually required for new life to emerge. When the trees release their leaves in autumn to enter winter's rest, the leaves fall to the ground and create mulch and compost, nutrition for the next cycle of life. I found that idea exhilarating.

Woodman says that the ego self must experience a kind of death where we release everything we have been clinging to, all the things we purport to value that are worthless. Those who embrace the wisdom of Kali, the dark goddess in Hinduism, "come to accept death as a necessary step in their transformations, then Kali can dance her dance of perpetual becoming. Once her cycles are accepted, those who love her are free of the fear of death, free of their own vulnerability, free to live her mystery."[6] The great mystery of Kali is that her destruction is in service to new creation. She is at the heart of the process of nature where leaves fall to make compost for future plant life. She is the letting go and death of autumn and winter that lead to spring.

Inanna's Journey as Archetypal

There are many ancient myths that describe the journey of descent into the underworld. One of the more significant is the story of Inanna, a Sumerian goddess (also known as the Babylonian Ishtar). Her journey offers an archetypal image of the descent as initiation, which includes the shedding of illusions, death and dismemberment, and rebirth. The Sumerian poem of Inanna's myth was probably created between 1900 BCE and 1600 BCE. She was the goddess of grains, fertility, war, love, healing, emotions, heaven, and earth. These stories of the underworld journey are archetypal, meaning they speak to an experience across cultures and to something deep in our psyches.

In the story, Inanna prepares to make a journey, adorns herself, gathers symbols for protection, and instructs her servant what to do in case she does not come back. When she arrives at the outer gates of the underworld, she announces herself as "Inanna, Queen of Heaven" on her way to see her older sister Ereshkigal, the queen of the underworld whose husband has died. When Ereshkigal hears her sister has arrived adorned rather than dressed for mourning, she becomes enraged and instructs the gatekeeper to seal the seven gates of the underworld and then open each one by just a crack, letting her through but demanding that at each one Inanna remove one of her royal garments as an act of humility.

Inanna agrees, stripping herself at each gate until she is naked to enter the throne room where her sister sits. There the judges of the underworld surround her and pass judgment against her. Ereshkigal gazes upon Inanna with the eyes of death, turns her into a piece of rotting meat, and hangs her from a hook on the wall.

Inanna is gone for three days and nights, and when she does not return, Inanna's servant begins to grieve and seeks out her grandfather and father for help, asking that they not allow their daughter to be put to death in the underworld. But both are angry with Inanna for her actions and refuse assistance.

Finally, the servant turns to Inanna's other grandfather, begging for help, and finds some compassion there. He creates two tiny creatures from under his fingernails and instructs them to enter the underworld like flies. Ereshkigal is in the midst of a deep lament over the death of her sister, and the two tiny creatures join her in her mourning. Once she feels heard, they ask her for Inanna's corpse. They then sprinkle the food and water of life on Inanna and she rises from death.

Before Inanna is allowed to leave, she is told she must provide a scapegoat, someone to take her place. Death will not be cheated. When she returns home, she finds her husband dressed in fine robes, oblivious to her absence, and she orders him to be taken away in her place. Her husband's sister cries out in grief and says she must share his fate. Inanna is moved by this and decrees that they each go to the underworld for half of the year, and each will spend half of the year in the world above.

This ancient story is of a spiritual initiation. Inanna's voluntary journey to the underworld and then surrender to being stripped of all her outward possessions seems to be a requirement across cultures for following this kind of path of descent. But she also prepares herself and asks for help and protection. Inanna's servant is symbolic of that part of us that stays above ground while the soul descends, the still-conscious aspect of the psyche that witnesses the events both above and below and holds compassion for the fate of the soul.

Ereshkigal can be seen as the shadow side of Inanna, the part of each of us that has experienced abandonment, fear, rage, greed, and loneliness. She experiences Inanna's light and beauty as achieved to some extent at her own expense and so responds out of anger and destruction. She also represents the energy of destruction in our lives, that which destroys all that is not our true Self or authentic calling in the world.

The descent to the underworld is through seven gates. Seven is a sacred number in many traditions, including Mary's Seven Sorrows, Catholicism's Seven Sacraments, or in yogic tradition, the seven chakras. These seven gateways we must all pass through on our own journeys of descent, and each demands a letting go of something that must be surrendered to move toward deeper initiation.

When Inanna enters the underworld, she receives judgment, the inevitable judgment of the external world against each of us, and her life is drained from her. She submits to pain and degradation, even death, to undergo the transformation. Sylvia Brinton Perera, in her book *Descent to the Goddess: A Way of Initiation for Women*, writes that in the underworld, suffering is the primary path.

> It is the place of the powerlessness of chaotic and numb or unchanneled affect, the lonely grief-rage of power-lessness and unassuaged loss and longing, a hellish place where all we know to do is useless (thus there is no known way out of the despair). We can only endure, barely conscious, barely surviving the pain and power-lessness, suspended out of life, stuck, until and if, some act of grace with some new wisdom arrives.[7]

This is the experience of impasse I wrote about in the previous chapter. This archetypal journey always brings us to a place of powerlessness, surrender, and a letting go of all the old ways we used to know of how to cope and move forward.

In Inanna's story, three days pass, which are traditionally viewed as the time of the dark moon, but we can also recall Jesus's time of death before his Resurrection as well. Three is another sacred number. Inanna had wisely relied on her inner witness and asked in advance for intervention and protection. Her servant seeks to find help but is at first rejected and then finally received with compassion.

The two tiny creatures enter the underworld to retrieve Inanna. They meet Ereshkigal in her suffering. The story affirms that this cry of grief is one voice of the dark goddess, a way of expressing the existence of things as they are, not necessarily seeking alleviation. Ereshkigal is so touched by their attention and presence that she offers gifts, and they ask for Inanna's rotting body and bring it back to life.

Ereshkigal places a demand on Inanna, though. She must follow the rules of the underworld and bring a substitute; she chooses the king who has not experienced any grief over her loss. His sister acts out of love and grief, not trying to flee or denigrate what is to be, and so she ends this pattern of scapegoating.

Making the Descent to the Underworld

The story begins by saying, "From the Great Above Inanna opened her ear to the Great Below,"[8] and in Sumerian, the word for *ear* and *wisdom* are the same. She turns toward the wisdom the underworld has to offer her. She also turns toward her own shadow side, symbolized by her sister. The journey involves stripping away the ego-identifications, defenses, old patterns, and illusions. It requires everything of us that we can possibly give, and sometimes more, until we have abandoned all external signs of our status and are simply ourselves, naked and alone. It can feel like being torn apart, and we don't always survive it. It is by necessity full of risk.

Many Indigenous cultures had rituals and community holding for such stages of dissolution. I often wonder if, in the Western world, such dissolution is so painful and dangerous at times because it lacks these communal containers for holding us in our experiences. We can draw upon this wisdom for our own underworld journeys, seeking the wisdom of elders who can help us navigate and create containers of holding to help sustain us.

This surrender of all our outer identities and identifications is a journey toward our own freedom and creativity. When we no longer fear what death can take from us, we can claim our own empowerment.

I invite you to also consider the way the world around us is making a collective descent into the underworld, one in which we must all participate. The sense of chaos and disruption of financial systems, the destruction of our natural world, racism, poverty, and global pandemic are all invitations to let go of the false securities we hold on to and to enter into a different way of being where we are more in touch with our own power, with our deepest call, with what is most essential to us. As a society we are being stripped of our most cherished collective beliefs about what makes life meaningful and valuable. There must be a collective descent before being reborn.

This is what the fierce dark feminine energy is about, this call to surrender into the forces and cycles of creation, to recognize ourselves as an integral part of following those rhythms, and how the destructive aspects bear wisdom for us and can ultimately lead to creation and new life.

What I find so beautiful about these images of the dark journey across traditions, cultures, times, and places is to know there is something archetypal about this experience. We cannot avoid it. The mystery of it is that if we surrender into it, let ourselves have the whole spectrum of the experience from its deep, gnawing ache to the sense of being torn apart, to the wrenching of the heart, it can be a journey of initiation and transformation. But I must repeat that it is also a dangerous road and there are no guarantees of coming through, especially unscathed or not undone. Elders, soul guides, and community are all essential. Nature is a wise teacher of this process. The journey of the butterfly is often a symbol of transformation because when the caterpillar enters the chrysalis, it completely dissolves before being formed anew.

Jesus and Mary Descend to the Underworld

There is a teaching in Christian theology called the harrowing of hell in Old and Middle English, or the descent of Christ into hell from the Latin, which refers to the period of time between Jesus's Crucifixion and his Resurrection three days later. The teaching is that Christ descended to bring liberation to the souls who dwelled there since the beginning of the world.

This descent into the underworld is referred to in the Apostles' Creed, where it says "he descended into hell." His descent is alluded to in the Christian scriptures in 1 Peter 4:6, which states, "For this is the reason the gospel was proclaimed even to the dead, so that, though they had been judged in the flesh as everyone is judged, they might live in the spirit as God does." The harrowing of hell is commemorated in the Christian liturgical calendar on Holy Saturday.

The Gospel of Matthew (12:40) also alludes to Jesus's descent: "For just as Jonah was three days and three nights in the belly of the sea monster, so for three days and three nights the Son of Man will be in the heart of the earth." Later in Matthew (27:50–54) it says:

> Then Jesus cried again with a loud voice and breathed his last. At that moment the curtain of the temple was torn in two, from top to bottom. The earth shook, and the rocks were split. The tombs also were opened, and many bodies of the saints who had fallen asleep were raised. After his resurrection they came out of the tombs and entered the holy city and appeared to many. Now when the centurion and those with him, who were keeping watch over Jesus, saw the earthquake and what took place, they were terrified and said, "Truly this man was God's Son!"

In the Hebrew Scriptures, the Jewish view of the afterlife was that whenever someone died, whether righteous or unrighteous, they went to Sheol, a dark, still place. However, in the Christian scriptures, there is a distinction between Sheol, which is regarded as the common place of the dead, and Gehenna, or the lake of eternal fire, where those who are condemned at the final judgment are sent. It is understood that Jesus descended into Sheol, rather than the hell of those who have been damned.

This descent also became the subject of artwork through the ages, including *Christ's Descent into Limbo*, a woodcut by German artist Albrecht Dürer, around 1510; *The Descent into Limbo* by Italian artist Andrea Mantegna in 1497; and *The Descent of Christ into Limbo* by Netherlands artist Pieter van der Heyden in 1561. All three of these images can be found easily with an online search. It is also a more common and prominent theme in Orthodox icons.

Similarly, there is some belief that Mary herself descended into hell after her death. Some medieval theologians believed that Mary's ability to intercede on our behalf reached all the way down to hell. Again, we are exploring hell as an archetypal reality in our lives rather than a literal place.

St. Anselm of Canterbury (1033–1109) praised the scope of Mary's power to save the condemned from hell and bring them to heaven: "O woman marvelously unique and uniquely marvelous through whom the elements are renewed, hell is redeemed, the demons are trampled underfoot, humanity is saved, and angels are restored."[9]

Because of Mary's sovereign power, depicted through names like Mary, Queen of Heaven, Queen of Angels, and Queen of Saints, it was believed she also had power over the devil. This image became popular in fourteenth-century England with her title Empress of Hell, which appeared in Medieval English carols, plays, and devotions. She also appears in some illuminated manuscripts of Books of Hours doing battle with the devil, including an image titled "The Virgin Mary Striking the Devil," which appears in *The de Brailes Hours*, circa 1240.

This is a very different image from Mary as passive virgin and then nurturing mother. She becomes a powerful force for change in her own right. When looking at medieval manuscript illuminations, one can find evidence that Christians put their hope in Mary for her direct intercession against Satan. Professor Vanessa Corcoran writes, "They were all part of a larger religious culture that viewed Mary's agency— her capacity to act of her own accord—as significant and complex."[10]

I find both images—Jesus and Mary descending into hell—compelling. If we consider hell to be an archetypal image of the struggles some people encounter both in this life and when they die, where some are unable to open to Love, then we might consider that both Mary and Jesus knew something of this underworld place and, like Persephone, were able to be present on behalf of the souls there. Their willing descent reveals an extraordinary compassion.

The underworld we experience is not always a feeling of hell, although the lack of security and knowing can often seem like it. There is consolation in knowing this reality is one visited by the divine presence. In those moments when I struggle the most, I can rest in knowing that neither Mary nor Jesus is afraid of the descent to the underworld, and they will meet me in that place.

Scripture Reflection by John Valters Paintner

The Crucifixion of Jesus

> *Meanwhile, standing near the cross of Jesus were his mother, and his mother's sister, Mary the wife of Clopas, and Mary Magdalene. When Jesus saw his mother and the disciple whom he loved standing beside her, he said to his mother, "Woman, here is your son." Then he said to the disciple, "Here is your mother." And from that hour the disciple took her into his own home. (John 19:25b-27)*

In the chapters leading up to this passage, Jesus goes from a dinner party with his closest friends to being abandoned by almost everyone he knows. Jesus is arrested after one of the apostles sells him out, and only one apostle attempts to stop the arrest. The chief priests, who arranged Jesus's arrest, turn him over to the Roman authorities. After a hasty trial, even the Roman governor washes his hands of Jesus, while outside the lone disciple to follow denies even knowing Jesus.

Jesus is made to carry his own cross to the place of execution outside Jerusalem. Through the very same city, where just days ago thousands of people were singing his praise, Jesus now walks with only a handful of followers there to witness to his execution. Once at Golgotha (the "place of the skull"), Jesus is crucified and a plaque is put above him announcing his crime against the state. While Jesus dies slowly on the cross, the soldiers divide his meager possessions.

From the cross, Jesus asks Mary and John (virtually the only people left in attendance) to be mother and son to one another.

The chapter, obviously, continues. But our passage today ends here. And the first thing I want to point out is that none of the evangelists record that Mary said anything during these events. Maybe watching her son be publicly executed was too much and she could do nothing but cry. Her lack of words here might be due to the misogyny that is prevalent throughout so much of scripture. Perhaps it was deference to her pain that what she may have said in anguish was not taken down for others to read or hear.

Another, perhaps more charitable, explanation is that the authors of the gospels wanted to keep the focus on Jesus. After all, Mary's last quoted words in the gospels were at the wedding feast at Cana where she turns to those around her and says, "Do whatever he tells you" (John 2:5b). From there, Jesus performs his first public miracle and embarks on his ministry. Mary birthed Jesus into the world and then sent him on his way to spread the Good News.

But this is where all that led: a mother watching her son die. But she is not alone. There are other women with her. There is also at least one disciple who stayed, despite the danger it may have placed him in. And while they may not be related by blood or marriage, Mary and John become family to one another (with all the rights and responsibilities, according to Jewish law).

Sorrow is always personal and often private. Mary may have wished for anonymity in those days. But her story teaches us that it need not be solitary. There can be great solidarity in pain. Not only was the apostle John asked to be a son to Mary in her time of sorrow, but also Mary was asked to be a mother to John in his sorrow.

What support do you have in times of sorrow?

Meditation

Encountering the Mother of Sorrows

Bring your awareness to your body; I believe very much that the disconnect from the sacred feminine is also related to our disconnect from our bodies and the disconnect from the earth. I strongly encourage you to connect with your bodies, not only because they are these vessels of holiness, but also because I think they help us to connect in an even greater way to the sacred presence of the feminine energies. In whichever way you identify your gender, we all have these different qualities or aspects in us. Become aware of your body and take a moment to bring some compassion to yourself. You might try placing your hands firmly on your forearms or thighs, which can feel really comforting and grounding. Feel yourself here, acknowledge your body, give it some loving touch. Then let your awareness drop back into the sanctuary of the heart.

We are inviting in the feminine face of the divine, however we might encounter that in our lives. If you have difficulty with that, go to your usual sense of divine presence and ask that presence for a more comfortable image to support you in maybe revealing a new face of the feminine sacred to you. This isn't something you have to force or make happen, but invite in an awareness of that presence of the holy mother, the life-giving mother, the compassionate one, the one who sits with us in our sorrows and our grief and our loss, the one who is a guide for us on the journey of descent, and the one who companions us through all of those heartaches and losses and stripping away. Ask that sacred presence to create a circle of protection around you.

Imagine there is a circle that will protect you from any presence that would wish you harm. It's also a way to consciously draw your energy and awareness back to yourself when it may be scattered in different directions as you begin. It's very much about intentionally turning back inward and honoring the inward journey as sacred. Allow yourself to be held by this compassionate divine presence holding a door open for you so that the feminine can be revealed to you in some new way. Invite this presence to walk with you through your life and to become aware of those moments of great sorrow that you have experienced. Wander through gently, and become aware of those times of doubt, of uncertainty, of despair.

Ponder those moments. Perhaps they are of illness or death of loved ones, the loss of jobs or income or security, betrayals from family or friends, or a deep pattern of dysfunction. Right now, we're not entering into each of these stories; we don't have to tell these stories to ourselves. We can just imagine we're opening up our arms and gathering those places of wounding into our arms, and welcoming Mary as the Mother of Sorrows to sit with us and help us to hold these stories.

If at any time your system feels overwhelmed, please pull back from the meditation and return to a safe holding space for yourself, and find something to bring you comfort.

What were those moments of sorrow that became some sort of initiation for you into a deeper maturity or wisdom, or into a deeper sense of how life can be pulled out so easily from under you? What were those loss-of-innocence moments, particularly the ones that may have gone unhealed?

Sit with this sacred feminine presence to hold these sorrows and shower yourself with her boundless compassion. Know that each one of us has a collection of griefs and losses that have shaped us into who we are. Bring some reverence and respect for having survived.

Ask this sacred feminine presence for her wisdom. Ask, how did she heal from her own seven great sorrows in life? What wisdom does she want to offer to you? Take a moment to listen and receive. How have they shaped who she is? What does she want you to know? Receive a gift that she has to offer to you, a symbol of this holy wisdom she gives to you about how to be with the sorrows of life. Receive whatever that gift might be.

Even if nothing appears, sit with gratitude in that emptiness. See if there's a gesture or a shape your body might take as an expression of this gift she gives to you. Then thank her for her presence, remembering that you can call upon her at any time. You can begin a practice of building a relationship with this aspect of the sacred feminine if you haven't already. Then offer gratitude to her, very gently begin to deepen your breath, and slowly bring your awareness back to the room that you're in.

Creative Exploration

Expressive Arts Unfolding
I offer a gentle reminder, as always, to bring any resources you need to support you in this experience. Use whatever materials you have available, and feel free to adapt this sequence as needed or desired.

You will be invited to create an altar, so spend a little time ahead gathering things like a colorful cloth, a candle, icons, a photo, and sacred symbols or objects from nature. More instruction is provided below.

Centering
Begin with centering. Connect to your breath. Allow your breath to bring your awareness down to your heart (one to two minutes).

Plant the Seed with Some Questions
- Where in my life have I encountered the archetype and energy of the dark feminine?
- When have I been asked to make a journey of descent, stripping myself bare along the way?

Connect to Your Body
Find a piece of music and become present to your body's wisdom and longing. How does your body want to move today? Move with the intention of releasing any kind of certainty or control. Follow what wants to emerge instead.

Creating an Altar
Find a small space in your home to create an altar for the midwinter journey as a way to continue to support you in making space for

the unresolved grief you carry and all the ways the world brings sorrow into your life. Spend some time reflecting on what has been most supportive to you in these weeks. Perhaps you put a cloth down in a color that reminds you of grief being held, or maybe a candle; perhaps include a stone or other nature object that helps you to remember to let nature carry your grief with you, or maybe an icon of Mary as Mother of Sorrows. You might include a photo of a loved one who has died. Let this process unfold over the space of several days, but you can set the intention during this creative exploration. Ask that symbols reveal themselves to you.

Writing Exploration: The Seven Sorrows of Your Life

Begin by connecting to a resource that can soothe and support your heart before revisiting the Seven Sorrows of Mary I shared earlier:

The prophecy of Simeon (that a sword would pierce her heart), the flight into Egypt, the loss of Jesus in the Temple, meeting Jesus while carrying the cross, the Crucifixion, Mary receiving Jesus's body, and Mary placing his body in the tomb.

Allow a few moments to imagine each of these events in Mary's life and enter into the suffering with her. Allow yourself to be fully present to Mary in these experiences so you can create a connection with her in grief and discover a kindred spirit in suffering.

Then, I invite you to begin contemplating the Seven Sorrows of your own life. Invite Mary to be present with you in this process, as you just did in her suffering. Perhaps there have been more or less, but seven is a sacred number, so I will suggest you begin there and then discern what number best expresses the great sorrows you have experienced. What have been the great, heartbreaking experiences of your life that have shattered you or made you come undone? Does your altar spark any memories? If you find you need to support and resource yourself, feel free to step back from this reflection at any time and give yourself what you need.

Give each of the sorrows a title or name of some kind so you can easily identify it if you return later to these reflections. Make a commitment to spend some time grieving for these losses in the coming weeks.

Silence

At the end, allow one or two minutes to rest into silence, letting go of all the words and images that have come. This is a time of integration, allowing your body and soul to integrate what has been stirred up in the process.

Questions for Reflection

- What are the ways that you respond to the needs of others while ignoring your own?
- Where has your own fear of growing older or dying created resistance or suffering in you?
- What are the ways you embrace the efficient and linear perspective on how things should be done in the world? And how might you begin to resist this in your daily life?
- How are you doing in this tender space of paying attention to grief and struggle?
- How are you holding yourself in the remembered ache of the heart?
- Where do you see your own journey reflected in Inanna's descent?
- Were there moments of recognition? Or perhaps resistance?

Retreat Participant Poems

My Seven Sorrows

Cynthia Gallo Callan

Sorrow
washes over me
as does the tide
on shells and stone.
My lady is beside me

whispering
you are not alone.

Sorrow
has me spiraling
down to where
I do not want to be.
My lady is beside me
whispering
that sorrow helps me see.

Sorrow
is deeply buried
in places I never
thought to look.
My lady is beside me
whispering
it's okay to be mistook.

Sorrow
opens wounds
which I thought
were truly healed.
My lady is beside me
whispering
self-forgiveness is what shields.

Sorrow
can be cleansing
to those memories
so long ago.
My lady is beside me
whispering
no longer are they my foe.

Sorrow
is acceptance
in the journey
when visited with grief.
My lady is beside me
whispering
it's not a sign of unbelief.

Sorrow
offers me a chance
to lend another
my hand.
My lady is beside me
whispering
so all will understand.

Hillel's Seven Sorrows

Hillel Brandes

- Childhood home (and beyond) seemingly without love
- "You don't matter"—my internal mantra of 5 decades
- Ending of a marriage of nearly 3 decades
- Only knowing a "False Self" (for 5 decades)
- Loss of an unborn child
- Not knowing to what I belong (for 5+ decades)
- Loss of community

6

THE TRANSFORMATIVE
MYTHIC JOURNEY

Myth is about vertical imagination. Myth opens up the connections we have to the heavens and the connections we have to the underworld. . . . On the surface a myth is false, but it carries deeper truths than you can find anywhere else.

–Michael Meade

The dark goddess is demanding. She is fierce, and if I surrender my ego's need for control, I go to meet a reality that turns my life upside down. She demands that I let go of my desire to direct the journey and allow a soft tenderness in me to come forth; she is the one who will transform me; she is the one who will allow the wild, sacred energy to work through me.

There are some parallels here between the dark goddess energy and the dark night of the soul experience. This call to a complete act of letting go of all securities, illusions, comforts, and idols is the path of darkness. It is always in service to wholeness, although the reality is that we may not survive our dark night journey. It is full of terror because the danger is very real.

I find a great deal of hope in these parallels. This journey of being thrust into the underworld by forces far greater than ourselves is a common mythological theme found in many cultures. The descent is sometimes a voluntary one in search of a deeper goal, or sometimes involuntary, when the abyss drops open beneath our feet. The potential and promise emerge either way from the fact that our ordinary ego perceptions are shattered and our well-crafted personas begin to crack. Here something new can emerge.

123

I believe that the conscious underworld journey we are called to take is a journey of initiation in service to our true calling, our deepest, most authentic selves and desires. When we are able to face this reality for ourselves, we are able to companion others in this as well.

Whatever the origin of our midwinter experiences, they are an invitation to do the painful work of letting go of what gets in the way of living our deepest call and embracing that which has been rejected within us.

The Archetype of the Orphan

We move now into archetypes as a support for this midwinter journey. We began exploring them in the last chapter through the dark feminine, images of the holy mother, and the journey of Inanna's descent. One of the things that is so powerful about archetypal energies is that they appear across time and cultures, so there is a sense of deep connection and universality. We are not alone in our experience.

Orphans appear across myths, fairy tales, and popular culture— think of Little Orphan Annie, Cinderella, Dorothy in *The Wizard of Oz*, and Harry Potter. Something about the Orphan speaks to us. Even the biblical story of the banishment from the Garden of Eden is a primal Orphan myth, as is the story of Jesus's experience of abandonment on the cross.

The Orphan archetype in each of us is activated by all the experiences in which the child in us feels abandoned, betrayed, victimized, neglected, or disillusioned. We are all orphaned in one way or another simply because we are raised by parents or caregivers with their own wounds, and somewhere along the way they have not been able to fully meet our emotional or physical needs—we *each* have an inner Orphan. We have each experienced abandonment in our times of need, and this is imprinted in us in a deep way.

I have this vivid memory from when I was less than two years old of trying to climb out of my crib on my own and hoisting myself onto the edge of the barrier that was holding me in. When I reached that point, my young heart suddenly panicked because I felt I was going to fall off the edge on the other side, and I started to cry and scream. My parents came in and found it all very amusing and even took a photo of me, which I still have, and only then put me safely back in the crib. But those few moments when my cries went unheeded have stayed with me as the first memory I have of being orphaned, at least in this archetypal sense. And despite my parents' many other wounds and addictions, I don't believe in that moment they were *trying* to be cruel. They probably figured they would catch me if I fell. Yet I experienced a profound sense of abandonment and, like all of us, many more to follow. You might have your own originating story when you first encountered your inner Orphan.

The work of being with our inner Orphan is to really feel its pain and abandonment. It is best when we can do this hard work from a place of strength and feeling good rather than waiting until we feel awful and plunged into abandonment again; however, this isn't always possible. So it is important to recognize that we each carry this energy in ourselves, even if it isn't being immediately activated. Healing begins when we feel the pain and reality of our orphaning experiences and allow the emotional response to move through us, and then progresses to recognizing how we have denied part of ourselves. Healing continues when we seek kindred souls to journey with us, when we build containers of holding for our experiences, and when we bring compassionate awareness to old patterns.

In addition to abandonment comes disillusionment, and yet this can be a gift in its own way when we let go of illusions we have been holding on to. Perhaps out of our Orphan experience, we have come to believe that we can never rely on anyone else for help and part of the journey is to shatter that illusion and find connection once again.

The journey of healing this archetype is to learn to nurture and care for ourselves and to discover our kinship to others who also experience the inner Orphan. Often Orphans feel like exiles and long for an experience of being at home. Remember Dorothy's words at the end of *The Wizard of Oz* as she clicks her heels together: "There's no place like home." That story is about the journey of the Orphan to discover that home is always with her. In that moment, she shatters the illusion that she is ultimately abandoned and left to her own devices. Returning home means remembering that there is a source of eternal love and compassion within each of us that is always available to us.

Each archetype has a shadow side and a light side. The shadow of the Orphan is this perception of complete powerlessness and being alone. It often shows up in cynicism. Originally betrayed by others, Orphans often betray their own hopes and dreams because they expect disappointment and then end up abandoning themselves again and again. The Orphan may do something to provoke rejection simply to have a greater sense of control over life. Since disappointment, rejection, and abandonment are seen as inevitable, we feel just a bit better by leaving first. Ironically, the more we live false, inauthentic lives in order to be safe from hurt, the more orphaned, hurt, and disillusioned we become. We have essentially turned against ourselves. Or we are unable to truly experience our own grief and integrate it.

The light side of the Orphan is the realization of our interdependence with one another. Often those who identify strongly with the Orphan are highly intuitive because they have suffered so much. This intuition and the empathy that comes from being present to our own suffering often leads to work in the healing field with others. This is the source of the "wounded healer" image that Henri Nouwen writes so beautifully about. We also begin to free ourselves from reliance on an external authority to find our own value but learn to be interdependent and join in mutuality with others who are as orphaned as we are. This archetype is connected to the power of the Sovereign (which I will explore briefly later in the chapter) and the call to not rely solely on others to meet our own needs but name them for ourselves and take care of ourselves when necessary and without apology.

To the degree that we do not acknowledge the Orphan inside us, that Orphan is abandoned by us as well as the world. Every time we judge ourselves for our experiences and feelings, we also abandon ourselves again. When we start to bring ourselves fully present to the pain and suffering, we begin the journey of healing this tender part.

Embracing our own Orphan archetype is a powerful way to break through our carefully built defenses, the way we deny our pain or our shadow. It offers us an image for our most fundamental realities of attachment and abandonment, of loss and loneliness. It is only when we welcome these parts of self in with compassion that we can begin to heal and live fully.

Ultimately, the Orphan learns that it is a source of power to face one's victimization and limitations and to feel fully the pain caused by them. Doing so frees us up to work together to create a better world. As I have mentioned before, bringing consciousness to these dark energies is a form of initiation, bringing us closer to our own deep wisdom.

When we become fully conscious of our orphanhood, this is a critical stage in our development—to be willing to become interdependent with others whom we recognize to be wounded just like ourselves. We enter into solidarity with the other Orphans of the world.[1]

The Archetype of the Destroyer

We have already encountered this archetype in the previous chapter on the fierce goddess who both destroys and creates—destruction in the service of creation. The Destroyer archetype lives within each of us. Ultimately, it is a source of tremendous power. It is that energy that we have seen in Christianity through the dark night journey and through the desert elders' stripping away of comfort and security. We hear the call each year on Ash Wednesday as we enter Lent and ash is rubbed on our foreheads; that tangible reminder of our mortality and the words "from dust you came and to dust you shall return" are uttered. We hear the cries of lament emerging from the psalms and Jesus hanging in agony on the cross, uttering those words of devastation: "My God, my God, why have you abandoned me?" We might hear the echoes of the Orphan here as well.

In the mythic tradition, we experience it through the fierce goddess who demands that we lay aside all of our ego attachments, descend into the underworld, and allow everything about which we feel certain to be destroyed. This was Inanna's journey, which we explored in the previous chapter.

The challenge is how to make space for this energy in each of us, this force beyond us that makes these demands. How do we welcome in the Destroyer and not become obsessed by it or seduced into thinking this is the only energy at work in our lives?

Carol Pearson, in her book *Awakening the Heroes Within*, writes:

> The void the Destroyer leaves in its wake is more pro-
> found and debilitating than the abandonment experi-
> enced by the Orphan. . . . The Destroyer assaults the
> successfully created persona and in the best cases makes
> way for something new. In the case of some mystics, the
> destruction makes way for the sacred, and they never go
> back to anything resembling their former life.[2]

The mystics who have experienced the dark night, and released their attachments to their images of God and how they think the world works, have encountered this archetypal energy of destruction in the service of rebirth.

The challenge is to enter the space of complete unknowing, or releasing any carefully constructed plans or ideas we have about how things are or should be. The Destroyer wants to rip our illusion of control from our grasp. Ultimately, the call of the Destroyer is for us to relinquish anything that is not necessary so that we may encounter our deepest selves. The virtue associated with the Destroyer is humility. Vulnerability is necessary.

In our experiences of profound loss or pain, we discover that every-thing we have counted on or tried to build toward has crumbled. Our foundations of belief in how the world works unravel. You do all the right things and still you suffer. Our theological frameworks come undone; our sense of meaning and purpose, our grounding, all seem to slip away. We experience chaos rather than order. Welcome to Job's world, that enigmatic book of wisdom that never directly answers the question of why we suffer but invites us into the experience.

We want to know that God will keep us safe from danger on our own terms, but opening ourselves to an encounter with the mysteries almost always requires an encounter with fear and recognition that the reality of the universe is not pretty and neat and in human control. We experience powerlessness. We are forced to give up attachment to everything inessential. We may even be forced to give up attachment to things that feel pretty essential and then see if we do indeed survive.

We are permanently changed by an encounter with the Destroyer. It can feel like dismemberment. The Destroyer will visit us again and again. It is part of the fabric of human experience. The suffering the Destroyer brings is not about blame but about the creation of meaning and encountering our deepest selves. Pearson goes on to write, "At some point in our lives, the Destroyer within or without strikes, and hollows us out, humbles us. It 'wounds' us and through that opening we are able to experience new realities."[3] Ultimately, the Destroyer is also the transformer and brings us closer to truth, to what is most meaningful and alive. The Destroyer calls us to enter this paradox.

Pearson describes the Destroyer as an ally "when we recognize the need to change or give something up without denying the pain or grief involved. The Destroyer can also become our advisor, for we can learn when making every major decision to consult our deaths. If we allow death—rather than our fears and ambitions—to guide us, we make fewer frivolous decisions. If you were going to die tomorrow, what would you choose today?"[4]

The Destroyer tries to dismantle the ego's grasping in service of the soul, but in the shadow side of this archetype, it is the other way around. The soul is destroyed in service to the ego's needs and demands. If we turn away from full presence and witness to this archetype, it can be subverted into addiction and all the ways we numb ourselves from life's pain.

The problem is that we so often resist or deny the Destroyer's presence that its power becomes subverted. Sometimes it is turned inward so we live in self-destructive patterns, which becomes the shadow side of this archetype. Sometimes it is turned outward so that we begin to undermine others in our lives, or care little of the impact of our lives on the earth. On a grander scale, we see the shadow of the archetype alive and well in governments and institutions that are unconscious of their own power. We can use this energy pathologically and engage in acts of self-destruction, murder, and rape—all perversions of this power. The shadow also reveals itself in an ongoing cynicism about life and an abiding despair.

Death as a Wisdom Teacher

We live in a time when we fear growing older; we are afraid of death. What would it be like to live in a culture where the wisdom of elders was deeply honored so that in growing older we knew that what we had to surrender in terms of physical health and vitality could be replaced with deep wisdom and a vibrant spiritual life? What would it be like to live in communities where death was regarded as a sacred threshold, and accompanying the dying on their final journey, a holy responsibility? I remember several years ago working with a woman in spiritual direction who was dying of cancer. Her last mission was to convince the hospital that the "dying rooms" should be as beautiful and comfortable as the "birthing rooms" she had seen.

St. Benedict writes in his Rule, "Keep death daily before your eyes." St. Ignatius, in one of his meditations in the Spiritual Exercises for making a good discernment, counsels a person to imagine they are on their deathbed and to reflect back on their decision from this perspective. What is revealed? St. Francis called Death his sister, revealing an intimacy and companionship.

The poet Rainer Maria Rilke believed Death was a vital companion who serves a necessary purpose of plunging us into the wondrous depths of life. "Death is our friend precisely because it brings us into absolute and passionate presence with all that is here, that is natural, that is love."[5] This is about not just physical death but all the losses and letting go throughout our lives.

Embracing the gifts of winter is in part about honoring Death and the return to the earth for deep rest as an essential part of the cycle of creation and restoration. Confronting our own mortality—which so often happens at midlife when our remaining years are less than what we have lived—puts life into a different kind of relief. Concern about image and achievements begins to fall away. We may begin to ask what our lives are truly about and begin to make serious choices about where to commit our time and energy.

Jungian analyst James Hillman writes that it is the work of the soul to reflect on the reality of our mortality: "What is human is frail, subject to death. To be human is to be reminded of death and have a perspective informed by death. To be human is to be soul-focused which in turn is death-focused. Or to put it the other way, to be death-focused is to be soul-focused."[6] This is not a morbid preoccupation but a genuine honoring of the giftedness of the time we have, the grace in that, the unknowing of when our time will end, and how, when we do remember our limited time, it can often have the effect of helping us to really reflect on and recommit to what is most important in our lives. This is one of the gifts the Destroyer archetype can bring to our lives when we open our eyes to the grace of our limitations.

The Archetype of the Sovereign

Sovereignty is about being centered in your own power and taking full responsibility for meeting your needs. Sovereignty sounds so archaic in some ways. And yet it is one of the archetypal energies we find within us. The reason so many myths and fairy tales speak of kings and queens is that these figures reflect back something of ourselves.

As 2010 began, I listened for a word to carry me through the year, something to challenge me and deepen into. I knew Sovereignty was calling to me. It was the year I turned forty, which felt significant, but

in a sense of being pressed up against my heart's deepest desires and
a call to really reflect on how I wanted to live the next forty years with
even greater intention and integrity. Sovereignty is in many ways a
midlife word. We don't really begin to live into our own power until
we have grown wise enough to recognize our limitations as well. In her
book *Queen of Myself: Stepping into Sovereignty at Midlife*, Donna
Henes suggests that the traditional stages for women of maiden, mother, and crone are incomplete as our lifespans get longer. She suggests
the addition of the queen or Sovereign archetype between mother and
crone as a time to really live into a sense of your own power. In the
book *King, Warrior, Magician, and Lover*, the King is described as a
primal energy in men's spirituality.[7]

The Sovereign accepts full responsibility for his or her choices in
life. One of the central questions is "what is my task in this world?"
Living into what that is may take a lifetime, but the Sovereign helps
us to claim the call that is our birthright and step into life with confidence. That gift is then offered with joy as a blessing to the world. No
apologies need to be made for offering this essential contribution. Our
inner Sovereign knows that the world will not be complete without our
part of the greater vision. We participate in the cocreation of a more
just and beautiful future, each in our own unique way. We manifest the
Sovereign's energy through centeredness, confidence, and calmness.

When I live from my inner Sovereign, I act out of a sense of agency,
which is a willingness to take action on my own behalf for the benefit
of others, to exert my power or influence. This is not what we think
we should be doing for others but something that emerges from the
very deep and wise place within us. My task is never determined by
"shoulds" or shame. I take full responsibility for choosing this path, and
there is a sacramental quality as it is a response to a holy calling. We
move away from a sense of victimization that can come with suffering
and realize we have a choice in how we respond to life.

Later in this chapter, John will explore the story of the Ascension.
Theologian Walter Wink says that "the ascension is not a historical fact
to be believed but an imaginal experience to be undergone."[8] It is about

not the record of facts but the transformation of power. He describes the Ascension as Jesus entering the archetypal realm. Jesus becomes one with the divine, entering into the fullness of his power and offering us a vision of what that power looks like for each of us. Ascension is in part about connecting to the Source and living from that power so that we might contribute to changing the world. When we live from our own sense of power, we encourage others to do the same simply by the way we act in the world.

How are you being called to take responsibility for your fulfillment in life and choices (even the unconscious choices you make that mean you aren't spending as much time on your passion as you'd love)?

The shadow side of the Sovereign is revealed in the tyrant, wielding power over others. It is traumatizing to have our power taken away by others, whether by individuals who were supposed to care for us or by institutions or governments that manipulate power to keep us disempowered. If we have experienced this regularly in our lives, power can be experienced as threatening due to its abuses.

Healthy humility is an essential aspect of the Sovereign, so when that is absent, we see the shadow emerge and overidentify with power for its own sake. Is there a "tyrannical" aspect to one of your inner selves? A voice that shuts out all others? The Sovereign is the source of our desire and movement toward greatness, but the shadow side can come through inflation and grandiosity. We have to recognize our proper relationship to this power. There is a healthy humility that must accompany it.

Another shadow side is the martyr who often lives out of a false humility. When we don't take responsibility for meeting our own needs and living fully in the world, we may start to feel resentful of others as we rely on them to meet our needs. We may resent someone who is living a full, glorious, and powerful life because it is what we so desperately long for. Are there times when you criticize someone else's gifts because of your own misplaced sense of responsibility? How do you seek approval from other people before taking care of yourself? Do you deny yourself the pleasures of life out of a misguided sense of sacrifice or unworthiness? Do you hold back on your enjoyment of life?

When we are baptized, we are given a white garment that marks us as sharing in Jesus's identity as priest, prophet, and king (Sovereign). The stories of resurrection call us to a new way of life and being in the world.

A true Sovereign blesses others by their presence. When we live into our own power in healthy and life-giving ways, we witness to a different way of being that empowers those around us. When we encounter someone who is deeply in touch with their Sovereign, it does not matter their wealth or status in the world; we listen because they are in touch with their own wisdom and are not afraid to speak it aloud. Sovereigns create safe and healthy spaces for others to grow and develop their gifts and are never threatened by others living into their own power as well. Our world needs people of maturity, centeredness, wisdom, and peace to help us move into the next phase of our evolution together.[9]

Persephone and the Journey from Victimhood to Sovereignty

I wrote earlier about my experience in 2010 of visiting Vienna and ending up in the hospital with a pulmonary embolism.

The days that followed this experience were filled with sweetness and grief. I kept seeing myself walking all those miles through the city, marveling that I had not collapsed and died alone on the street.

The month before I went on this trip, our beloved dog Petunia had to finally be put to sleep after weeks of declining with canine dementia, and my mother-in-law had entered hospice because of her Alzheimer's. It was indeed the season of winter.

I began to ponder the story of Persephone, one I had always been drawn to because of the underworld descent and because of its connection to the seasons of the year.

I suddenly saw the story in a new way. Persephone is abducted into the underworld by Hades; she is the victim, torn away from her mother and the life she knew. When the story begins, she is a young maiden gathering wildflowers in a meadow, and the earth beneath her opens and swallows her up. There is much negotiation among the gods as to how to secure her return. She is an Orphan as the story tells of her abduction, a victim of Hades's force, and abandoned to the will of others. She encounters the Destroyer as everything is stripped away. She longs for her mother intensely. She has been removed from everything familiar.

In *The Long Journey Home: Re-visioning the Myth of Demeter and Persephone for Our Time*, Christine Downing writes: "Being taken to those depths is always an abduction. For we—or, at least, I—never feel quite well enough, quite courageous enough, quite mature enough to go *there* on our own. We are always still virginal before the transformative experiences."[10] We feel abducted because we would never wish for nor desire this experience.

Eventually she is allowed to leave, but because she has eaten some pomegranate seeds, she must return to the underworld for part of the year, which is when her mother Demeter goes into mourning and the world returns to winter. In some versions of the story, she is tricked into eating the seeds, but in others she has eaten them willingly and knowingly. I prefer to believe the latter. At some level, even though she entered the underworld as victim, in this act of choosing to eat the pomegranate seeds, she transforms herself from victim to queen. Persephone then becomes known as the queen of the underworld. She has been transformed, and her experience of abandonment and undoing leads her to loving service on behalf of the souls arriving there. The healing journey is always from Orphanhood to Sovereignty. We slowly learn to claim our own power not by denying our wounds but by finding the treasure there. It is the journey of a lifetime. Her role is to welcome in the new souls and guide them in their time of disorientation and transition.

There is a power we are each called to claim during our own dark journeys. Certainly we have all been victimized by life in one way or another: we have our own abductions; we have all had things happen we wish never had, traumas we carry that continue to wound us. We can continue to be victimized by our stories again and again; we can continue the vicious cycle of betrayal and abandonment upon ourselves by cementing ourselves in these patterns. Or at some point, we can make a choice to claim the winter journey as a source of power as well as pain. We can step into our inner Sovereign who dwells alongside the Orphan and Destroyer and a myriad of other energies we each carry. The fullness of the Sovereign is no longer victim; she knows what she needs and meets those needs without apology to others. She chooses to stay present to the underworld experience because she knows that by not running away, she finally arrives fully in herself. She embraces the deep mysteries as integral to life's journey. This is essential to the journey toward full spiritual maturity.

Downing writes, "But time spent in Hades that is not spent desperately trying to get out also leads to the discovery of the power and beauty of dark moments in our life, the real confusions and desolations. Fear is so different when one does not have to fear fear but can simply *fear*, incompleteness and hurt are also different when one sees them not as something to get beyond but as something to live."[11] There is so much grace in allowing our emotions to have room within us, rather than resisting them. We can meet fear with compassion, rather than fear of the fear. This helps to transform the experience into one where we can reclaim our power.

This has parallels to the dark night of the soul. Once we relinquish the need to move through on our own timelines and surrender to the wisdom of what is unfolding, even as it demands every last ounce of endurance we might have, this is precisely where the transformation happens.

We can welcome fear in with compassion and gentleness, and simply be with the pain and hurt, and see how our resistance multiplies the pain and often leaves us stuck. The shift in my own awareness of the story came from this insight into Persephone's claiming her queenship right in the midst of this underworld, as well as the awareness of all the ways in the past I had tried to be present to my midwinter journey while simultaneously hoping it would soon be over. This is a natural response, but the real opening happens when we stop trying to get beyond the dark night and enter fully there, once and for all. It is not the last word of the story, but this subtle living for what is next still keeps us from making the full descent. And it is the full descent that is required for resurrection to happen. The paradox is that we can't descend hoping for the new life that follows; we have to enter the darkness on its own terms and allow it to strip us of all securities.

Marion Woodman describes how our suffering is a sign that we are cut off from the great myths that give meaning to these experiences: "One reason people are suffering today to an almost intolerable degree is that their unmediated suffering has no conscious connection with its archetypal ground. Cut off from that ground they feel they are alone and their suffering has become meaningless. They do not realize that what they are suffering exists within creation itself and that the gods and goddesses of religion and mythology have been there before."[12] Myths offer us maps of the movements of our inner life, offering us meaning and purpose in the dark journeys we are compelled to make. The experience of emptiness is often gestation, bringing something wondrous and holy to birth into the world.

We are called to make a conscious descent into the underworld, not to stay there, but to travel through and make friends with the darkness and let its wisdom gestate within us. Ultimately, the deeper call is to carry that wisdom back into the world in generative ways.

In his book *Persephone Unveiled*, Charles Stein writes:

> Persephone is an aspect of every person, male or female, and her ravishment is the relation of the individuated soul to a darkly numinous background that is the shadow of death itself, the overwhelming character of an aspect of Being that, though beyond identity, is still irrevocably intimate with what one is.[13]

The call is to become one who has entered into full union with the chaos, who has embraced Death as the sister St. Francis tells us she is and not turned away. This is not something we achieve overnight; it is a long journey of practicing staying awake. We need to be resources for the journey; we need companions who have been through the journey themselves.

I believe that if we held a deep respect, rather than rejection, of these dark night and underworld experiences of incubation and mystery, if we stopped resisting the call to let go and transform, the experience might not be quite so frightening. If we spoke more freely about it in our churches, there would not be such a sense of loneliness and isolation when we endure it. We could gather communities of wise ones who have traveled the dark path before us. We could bring this power into the world to support others in their journeys to transformation and maturity.

Scripture Reflection by John Valters Paintner

The Ascension of Jesus

> Then he led them out as far as Bethany, and, lifting up his hands, he blessed them. While he was blessing them, he withdrew from them and was carried up into heaven. And they worshiped him and returned to Jerusalem with great joy; and they were continually in the temple blessing God. (Luke 24:50–53)

The previous chapter of Luke's gospel ends with a real sense of finality. Jesus has not only died on the Cross, but he is physically buried in a tomb behind a massive stone. But even in that detail there is a hint of more to come, as the complete burial ritual is interrupted by the Sabbath, and the women must return after it to finish anointing Jesus's body.

The next chapter begins early on the morning after the Sabbath. Several of Jesus's female disciples go to his tomb to anoint his body. But they find the tomb open and empty. They are startled by a figure in dazzling clothing. The figure asks them what they are doing, as they should know that Jesus is risen, just as he said he would. Remembering Jesus's words, the women run back to the rest of the disciples to tell them what they had seen. The apostles doubt them, and Peter runs to the tomb to confirm their story.

Next, we have the story of two disciples who are fleeing Jerusalem for Emmaus. Along the way a stranger joins them, and they discuss all that has happened the last few days. When the disciples stop at an inn for the night, the stranger makes to keep traveling. The disciples implore the stranger to stay and eat with them so that they may continue their conversation. Only in the breaking of the bread do the disciples finally recognize the risen Jesus who immediately disappears. The disciples are so overcome by the experience that they run back to Jerusalem that very night to tell the rest of the disciples whom they had met on the road.

Jesus then appears to the rest of the disciples who are shocked and afraid. But Jesus calms them and blesses them with peace. He shows them the wounds of his Crucifixion. The disciples' disbelief is replaced with great joy, and they offer him food that they eat together. After the simple meal, Jesus reminds them of his teachings, encouraging them to rest until the time for them to go forth into the world.

Finally, Jesus takes the disciples to Bethany. There he blesses them before ascending into heaven. The disciples pray there before returning to Jerusalem, overcome with joy.

Luke's gospel doesn't get into any details of what happens to Jesus or what he gets up to between his death and Resurrection. We just know, based on this text, that Jesus is back. Something significant obviously happened. He's changed. Even those who were closest to him often don't recognize him. It's not just that they doubt their eyes; they don't know who he is. And yet the core of who Jesus is doesn't change. He's still concerned for others. He greets people with words of calm and peace. He blesses them and reassures them.

Perhaps it's not that Jesus has changed at all but that the perception of others has changed. His disciples are finally seeing his true self. As Jesus ascends into heaven, Luke says that the disciples worship him. They are finally beginning to get it. They've now seen him rise from the dead and ascend to take his seat at the right hand of God, the Prince of Peace.

The disciples witness Jesus move more fully into his power. He is not a victim on a cross; his painful execution doesn't harden his heart or turn him against humanity, not even those who persecuted him. Instead, Jesus is transformed into a Sovereign and offers the continued gift of his presence to help empower others. He shows the way for us to live from our truest, deepest, fullest self; we can overcome the tremendous challenges life gives us and extend ourselves in compassion to others.

Meditation

End-of-Life Wisdom

I invite you to deepen your breath in a way that works for your body. Bring your awareness to your body. As you are breathing, begin to drop your awareness back inward, withdrawing your attention from the world.

Return to the sanctuary of the heart and invite in that source of infinite compassion, who can bathe you and all of the places of woundedness and hurting in love and care. You might offer some loving touch to your own body as a gesture of this holding in love. Ask the divine presence within you to help you create a circle of protection around yourself. Become aware of that sense of the divine presence in every direction around you, a boundary to help keep your presence and your attention focused inward.

Imagine in the sanctuary space that you have this gift of being able to see yourself at the very end of your life. Imagine that you are quite elderly and you are declining with something that isn't causing you too much pain, but people have gathered because they know that the time is near. There's a peacefulness to this death. But you're aware that the end is near and loved ones are coming to say goodbye.

Notice who it is that is showing up at your bedside at this threshold moment of the end of life. Listen to what each of those visitors and honored guests wants to say to you. What words of remembrance do they have to offer to you? What is it they want to uplift about who you are and who you've been in the world? Receive these words and images as gifts from your loved ones, from those who have gathered with you. Then allow some quiet so you can reflect on your own life.

Reflect back to this current season of your life from the perspective of being on your deathbed. As you reflect back, think about what the graces of your life have been. What have been the things you would let go of perhaps sooner than you did? What is it that you would want less of in your life? What are the things that could be stripped away, especially when you remember that your days are precious and few? What are the things that you want more of? What are the things you want to fill your days with? What are the things you want to be remembered for? How might you step more fully into your Sovereignty?

Become aware again of the circle of companions with you. You now see some companions who may not be still alive in this world. They may be those who've passed through the veil. They may be some of the saints and ancestors who have come to be with you. They don't have to be there in their physical presence. Know that as you stand at the final threshold of life, you are not alone.

Offer your present-day self one word of wisdom. What is one thing you want your present-day self to remember, to carry forward?

Take some slow breaths and very gently come back to the room and allow some time for reflection.

Creative Exploration

Expressive Arts Unfolding

Remember to use whatever materials you have available, and feel free to adapt this sequence as needed or desired.

Gather a piece of plain paper as your base, a glue stick, and old magazines or catalogs. I find that *National Geographic* works really well both for the diversity of images and the heavy paper they are printed on. Often used bookstores or libraries will sell old copies at a very low cost. You could also print images you find online or create a digital collage.

Centering

Begin with centering. Connect to your breath. Allow your breath to bring your awareness down to your heart (one to two minutes).

Plant the Seed with Some Questions

- Where do I encounter the archetypes of the Orphan, Destroyer, or Sovereign in my life?
- What are the situations where I feel a victim? What are some ways to reclaim my power?

Connect to Your Body

Find a piece of music and become present to your body's wisdom and longing. How does your body want to move today? Move with the intention of releasing any kind of certainty or control. Follow what wants to emerge instead.

Consider doing an online search for the traditional spiritual song "Sometimes I Feel Like a Motherless Child" for a musical evocation of your inner Orphan.

Collage Exploration

All you need for collage work is a blank piece of paper to glue your collage pieces on, a glue stick, and a source for images. This can be old magazines, catalogs, or even used art books.

As you look through the images you have available, keep the question in mind and be present to your inner responses. It is helpful to choose images that create any kind of energetic response in you, whether pleasant or unpleasant. Sometimes the images we resist the most can be the greatest teachers, as these often hold some aspect of our shadow life in them.

There are two ways to create a container for this process. The first is to limit the size of your base. You can choose to do a very small collage (say, four-by-four inches) or you can create something quite large if you have more time. Similarly, you can limit yourself to maybe three images and let that be enough, or if you have more time, choose several to work with.

Once the paper size and images have been selected, let the images tell you how they want to be arranged on the paper. After they are all glued down, spend some time speaking from each image through writing in a journal. It can be helpful to write "I am . . ." on your page and then speak from the voice of the image. These images and the voices they speak with will become the foundation for various characters in a story you are invited to write in the next section.

Writing Exploration: Fairy Tale

Consider writing your own fairy tale. Begin with "Once upon a time" and include your inner Orphan, inner Destroyer, and inner Sovereign as three of the main characters; then see where the story wants to take you. Add in other images or archetypes that emerged in your collage process. Fairy tales are powerful forms because we give expression to this deep archetypal truth in story form. Writing in third person can also offer us a powerful perspective on our story in a new way. Let the story tell itself. There doesn't have to be a "happily ever after" at the end.

Silence

At the end, allow one or two minutes to rest into silence, letting go of all the words and images that have come. This is a time of integration, allowing your body and soul to integrate what has been stirred up in the process.

Questions for Reflection
- Where do you feel most nurtured and cared for?
- How do you sabotage your own dreams because of fear of abandonment?
- How have your orphaning experiences been rites of passage, initiating you into a deeper wisdom?
- Vocation often arises out of woundedness—how has your ministry or service to the world been nurtured and brought to life by a core wound?
- How has the wounded healer been at work in your life story?

Retreat Participant Poems

A Fairy Tale

Inge Zwikker

Once upon a time, there was an orphan who tried very hard to Please everyone she met. She went out of her way to be good, get her As at school and be the Teacher's Pet. She just wished that she was her mother's (who also happened to be a teacher) pet. But her mother was a Critic, which is what parts of the Orphan learned to do too—to be harsh and judgmental on herself and everyone around her. Nothing was ever good enough, or even just enough. That is why the little girl was an orphan. She had no one else and she was alone most of the time. She felt Destitute and like she was begging for crumbs or pennies of love and attention anywhere she could get them. But it wasn't enough, and soon the wanting love and attention that didn't come from whence she needed it turned into Rage. Rage at the world, the universe, everyone and everything. Mostly this was stuffed down, only to erupt at unexpected times. Another belief formed. Not only was she not good enough but also she didn't belong here. This wasn't her world. She didn't fit in. She was out of place and lost. What planet should she be on instead? Maybe she accidentally got out at the wrong transit stop that said "Earth." Maybe someone pinned the wrong sign on her sweater, stating what her destination was supposed to be. One of the ways she tried to fit into the world was to take on more and more duties and responsibilities, much more than any child could realistically manage. She thought that if she took very good care of others, especially her mother, then maybe, finally, she would get bits of love. But it was all too much, and all she felt was the weight of the burden of Carrying Too Much. She tried so hard to please the world that she bought into all the pushing, driving, striving, achieving—a Whirlwind of activity that was empty and meaningless. She felt more and more Abandoned and lonely, betrayed and disillusioned. She just didn't get it. What was she doing that was so wrong? It must be really bad because awful things kept happening over and over, no matter how hard she tried. Feeling so Abandoned led to a lot of stress and trauma that eventually, over time, led to her becoming Sick. Being Sick destroyed what life she had been able to create for herself . . . which was kind of built on a false foundation anyways, so it didn't really count. So now, here she is, sick and traumatized and still trying to figure out how on earth to heal both these things. Maybe it can't happen on Earth. She has been trying hard for decades, to no avail. Is there ever—never—going to be any healing? Should she give up? But what if that means she dies? Her life seems to be full of trying too hard and having that go all wrong. What is she to do?

Lament of St. Brigid

Carla Shafer

Creator Spirit,
Source of breath and pulse,

How can you let families suffer?
Where are you when children

lose parents who care or are
torn from family and friends?

Cloaked with the belief
we must not interfere, blanketed
with fears that we can do nothing,
we let circumstances go unchanged.
We step aside—

Have mercy
Help us remember our childhoods
Restore us

In you all things are possible
Stir us to meet children's
needs. Embolden us with
your word. Breathe understanding
into us. Pulse steady through our
breaking hearts.

Bring a storm of peace
for all to weather and be renewed.

Conclusion

The darkness embraces everything,
It lets me imagine a great presence stirring beside me.
I believe in the night.

–Rainer Maria Rilke,
The Book of Hours

We have taken a long journey together through the gifts of the winter season, through the landscape of grief, the wisdom of Christian mystics like John of the Cross, the compassionate and fierce divine feminine, and the archetypes of Orphan, Destroyer, and Sovereign.

We have been opening ourselves here to create meaning out of life's pain. We must resist the temptation to offer easy or trite answers. We need to slow down and be with the suffering and loss before creating new stories. One of my favorite books on desert spirituality is *The Solace of Fierce Landscapes* by Belden Lane. He writes, "All theologizing, if worth its salt, must submit to the test of hospital gowns, droning television sets, and food spilled in the clumsy effort to eat. What can be said of God that may be spoken without shame in the presence of those who are dying?"[1] He goes on to write:

> My fear is that much of what we call "spirituality" today
> is overly sanitized and sterile, far removed from the
> anguish of pain, the anchoredness of place. Without
> the tough-minded discipline of desert-mountain experi-
> ence, spirituality loses its bite, its capacity to speak pro-
> phetically to its culture, its demand for justice. Avoiding
> pain and confrontation, it makes no demands, assumes
> no risks. . . . It resists every form of desert perversity,

147

> dissolving at last into a spirituality that protects its read-
> ers from the vulnerability it was meant to provoke. The
> desert, in the end, will have none of it.[2]

A life worth living engages with the pain of the world. Darkness can be a fertile ground for our growing wisdom and maturity.

One of my hopes is that through this work we have each discovered a fierceness—both within our image of the divine, the One who asks us to release all of our securities in the service of a deeper call and truth, and within us, that we might be fiercely present to ourselves and to those who come to us in their own dark nights, and resist offering false comfort and solace.

My other hope is that we have also discovered a radical tenderness toward ourselves and all the vulnerable places within. The more we bring compassion to these aspects of ourselves, the more we can bring that compassion to others as well.

Imagine what happens when we make room for everyone's midwinter journey: when we don't have to compare our suffering to others and our stories can be told freely, when we tell these ancient myths to one another so that we can remember we are not alone in the dark night, and when we create spaces and rituals that honor the transformative power of these times.

I believe many are seeking companions on the way who have done this kind of deep inner work, stood in the face of their own terror and not looked away. To be fierce when someone comes and offers me their own heartbreaking story is to not look away, to not try to rush them to meaning or light, and to let them be in the deep darkness knowing that I am standing witness.

To be fierce means not trying to sanitize or sterilize either our spirituality or the stories we must tell to make them more palatable.

This fierceness also extends to our work for justice in our communities. These threads of denial of the dark feminine are deeply connected to the exploitation of people and nature. Our own dark night journeys are always in service to the collective. The healing and meaning we find is to create a more loving and vibrant world.

Spiritual Maturity

Spiritual maturity comes through the long, slow process of staying awake to these realities, of entering the dark night experience again and again without demanding the transformation that can come only in its own time. It is about becoming slowly more aware of our own patterns of self-destruction or abandonment and then meeting ourselves with deep kindness and compassion. We are called to be open to the journey and not resist our experience.

A spiritual life and practice does not exempt us from the conditions of our humanity. It can't save us from suffering.

It is a challenge to learn how to be fully present to everything within us that brings grief, sorrow, rage, shame, and suffering. Many do not have the courage to abandon our relentless search for security. We have to embrace grief and pain as a condition of our humanity.

Fr. Ron Rolheiser writes:

> When you lose your securities, when you find yourself in an emotional and spiritual free-fall, when you are in the belly of the whale, let go, detach yourself, let the pain carry you to where it needs to take you, don't resist, rather weep, wail, cry, and put your mouth to the dust, and wait. Just wait. . . . Anything you do to stop what's happening will only delay the inevitable, the pain that must be gone through in order come to a new maturity.[3]

We can never demand the revelations that emerge from a conscious underworld journey, staying wide awake with the Destroyer, but we can give ourselves to the encounter with a willingness to be present, to show up fully. The qualities of waiting, cultivating, patience, endurance, and surrender are all essential for the process.

We must resist violence and oppression at every turn, but when we have experienced it, we must release our resistance to our experience. We must make space for the tender brokenness, for the sense of being unraveled and undone. Only by walking into this place as awake as we can be does it transform into power.

Revisiting Essential Practices

As we come to the end of this book, I want to revisit some of the practices we have explored in these pages and invite you to consider how you might make these a more central part of your life.

Somatic Resourcing Practice. Identify one or two things that help you to feel in this moment that you are okay. This can be something soothing that can calm down and help to regulate an activated nervous system if overwhelming experiences are present. These might include a hand on the heart, an object you can hold, or a blanket around you. Deepen your connection to this resource by revisiting it often, getting to know the physical sensations of it. I invite you to also notice what feelings or images arise in response to the resourcing, such as a sense of well-being even in the midst of turmoil, or a resource serving as an anchor in the storms.

Meditation. This is the practice of paying attention and staying awake. In meditation we cultivate our inner witness, that wise and infinitely compassionate aspect of ourselves. We need time spent in stillness to be with our thoughts and feelings; we need space to listen to what is happening within us, allowing it to move through us.

Art-Making. Creating visual art is a way of giving form and outward expression to deeply felt inner experiences. Carl Jung believed that we come to new insight first through symbol and only later through verbalization. Cultivating a practice of visual expression offers a place in our lives to be with the preverbal experience and give it honor. Tending our dreams is a similar practice of listening in this way.

Movement. I have found practices that reconnect me with my body in gentle ways to be very profound in my own healing journey. "Gentle" means titrating our movement, going slowly and within our physical and emotional capacity. Often when we experience trauma, we disconnect from our bodies and emotions. We have memories and feelings frozen in our brains that have not been expressed and that manifest in our muscles and body. Giving the body freedom to move how it longs to is another way of honoring those experiences that have yet to be accompanied by words. Practices like yoga and expressive dance can help to heal the wounds of abuse by giving us an experience of empowerment and strength.

Free Writing. This is when we write without editing ourselves and allow the free flow of ideas, feelings, symbols, dreams, and other possibilities through words. Journaling has been a close companion to me for the last forty years and has always been a place I could express my deepest longings and give it a safe container. Create rituals for writing and allowing what is unfolding in you onto the page.

Poetry. While poetry uses words, it does so in a way that distills the essence of an experience. Many times I have been "found by a poem" and discovered that a particular line lives on in me, revealing new insights. Poetry helps us to hold the tensions and paradoxes of life together, not dismissing either its struggle or its beauty. Both reading the poems of others and writing our own helps to support this process.

Ritual Space. We desperately need ritual spaces where lament can be expressed freely and fully, where we can cry out to God about the suffering we experience. We need meaningful rituals that help to mark our transitions into and out of the dark passage, honoring our courage in making a conscious journey and honoring our wisdom when we emerge.

Being in Nature. Forests and oceans remind us of our smallness; the humbling indifference of crashing waves or howling wind to our struggles can be a strange kind of solace, to be reminded that there are much bigger energies at work in the world. Or, as the poet Rainer Maria Rilke wisely writes, we can bring our grief and offer its weight back to the earth and back to the seas.

I encourage each of you to contemplate the place these practices might have in your life. These will help to offer companionship on the way and resources to draw upon when life feels torn apart again. You may have additional practices to add to this list.

Blessings to you as you journey forward. I delight in knowing that you have been traveling here for this season and all the ways you will bring this work to others. Even just being more present to those you sit with in the moments of darkness offers a new path in the world. I imagine that as we each make more and more space for the breaking down of things in our world, we are simultaneously holding the containers for the new possibilities to emerge on both individual and collective levels.

Questions for Reflection

- I invite you to reflect on your hopes and desires for this journey and exploration. Remember back to your longings when you opened this book. What have been the images, symbols, and metaphors that most resonated with you? Which ones did you most resist?
- Have you arrived where you thought you would?
- Have you had unexpected surprises? Gifts? Challenges?
- What do you most want your future self to remember?

Retreat Participant Poems

Untitled

Elaine Breckenridge

I found the fierce compassionate divine
in Earth's original monastery.
Descending into the depths of myself
angels, masquerading as birds sang of her arrival.

In Earth's original monastery
She sang the hymn of creation.

Angels, masquerading as birds sang of her arrival.
I knew I was made in her image.

She sang the hymn of creation.
Descending into the depths of myself
I knew I was made in her image.
I found the fierce compassionate divine.

Untitled

Lisa Palchick

The me I see in dreams is a painting
When shattered, images hold me
I enter into unknowing through art making
The Black Madonna holds my losses

When shattered, images hold me
The work of healing is ongoing
The Black Madonna holds my losses
I yearn for more God, all the time

The work of healing is ongoing
I enter into unknowing through art making
I yearn for more God all the time
The me I see in dreams is a painting.

Untitled

Denise Dale

Stability is a gift of Winter
Invitation to stay with Dark Night

Entering into hibernation and rest
Resisting the need to produce

Invitation to stay with Dark Night
Letting go of what I think I know
Resisting the need to produce
Allowing Divine into tender places
Letting go of what I think I know
Entering into hibernation and rest
Allowing Divine into tender places
Stability is a gift of Winter

I close this journey with a poem I wrote in honor of winter. Let it be a blessing for you as you continue onward.

Let It Be Winter Still

Christine Valters Paintner

Let it be winter a while longer,
Let darkness be my closest companion
cradling me in her inky velvet shawl.
Let the owl cry softly from his place
among the long aching branches,
under the bone-white face of the moon.
Let my heart break for the dead in Haiti,
buried under collapsed stone and wood
and the seeping river of death flowing underground.
Let me shed tears for widows and widowers
in Iraq and Afghanistan,
who must walk through each long day without the
warm calloused hand of their one true love.
Let me weep for the man dying less than a mile away,
alone as he reaches for that bright doorway.
Let me feel the gnawing sorrow of the woman

pressing her hungry children close against her body.
Let the winter stay a while longer.
Let her invitation to grief
carry me across the haunting threshold
to the places of my own great losses,
until I know this black frozen landscape as my own,
until the mournful songs of my ancestors vibrate in my blood,
wounded in wars, the grand kind, or the smaller battles of daily life.
Let the winter linger until I see each naked tree
as a talisman of my sorrow
and I long to be stripped down to my own essence,
reaching my arms up in supplication under a wide twilight sky.
Let it be winter until the moment the Hour of Spring
breaks through in laboring, gasping, heaving pains.
Until tiny miracles burst forth in an array of buds and blossoms
each one carrying a name: Love. Kindness. Compassion. Hope.
Each name earned only from the long barren journey of heartbreak.
Let it be winter still.[4]

Acknowledgments

This book is the fruit of many difficult and challenging times and learnings about the rich traditions of underworld and dark night journeys. Companions on this path have been essential, and I am extraordinarily grateful to my husband, John, and my spiritual director, Terry, as well as many dear soul friends.

Three of the Abbey of the Arts Wisdom Council members graciously read through this manuscript, attentive to issues on antiracism, antiableism, and trauma sensitivity. I want to thank Claudia Love Mair, Aisling Richmond, and Jamie Marich profusely for their contributions that infinitely enriched this book.

A deep bow of gratitude also goes to the many participants in previous online versions of this material. I always learn so much from those who choose to journey with me in this way. I am very thankful for those who were willing to share some of their writing that appears at the end of the chapters here.

Thank you, as always, to the wonderful team at Ave Maria Press and to my editor Isabelle Lahaie for the great support and enthusiasm for my work.

NOTES

INTRODUCTION

1. Richard Rohr, *Everything Belongs: The Gift of Contemplative Prayer* (New York: Crossroad, 2003), 45–46.

2. Stephen K. Levine, *Poiesis: The Language of Psychology and the Speech of the Soul* (London: Jessica Kingsley Publishers, 1997), xvi.

3. Miriam Greenspan, *Healing the Dark Emotions: The Wisdom of Grief, Fear, and Despair* (Boulder, CO: Shambhala Publications, 2003), 287.

4. Gwen McHale, "The Power of Containment," *Somatic Therapy with Gwen McHale* (blog), August 4, 2016, https://gwenmchale.word-press.com/2016/08/04/the-power-of-containment/.

5. McHale, "The Power of Containment," https://gwenmchale.wordpress.com/2016/08/04/the-power-of-containment/.

1. THE GIFTS OF WINTER AND DARKNESS

1. Barbara Brown Taylor, *Learning to Walk in the Dark* (San Francisco: HarperOne, 2015), 7.

2. Clark Strand, *Waking Up to the Dark: Ancient Wisdom for a Sleepless Age* (New York: Monkfish Book Publishing, 2015), 40.

3. Paul Coutinho, *Sacred Darkness: Encountering Divine Love in Life's Darkest Places* (Chicago: Loyola Press, 2012), 6, Kindle.

4. Perdita Finn, foreword to *Waking Up to the Dark*, by Clark Strand (New York: Monkfish Book Publishing, 2015), xiii.

5. Michael Meade, "Enlightenment Then and Now," *Living Myth* (podcast), https://www.mosaicvoices.org/episode-219-enlightenment-then-and-now.

6. Chet Raymo, *The Soul of the Night: An Astronomical Pilgrimage* (Cambridge, MA: Cowley Publications, 2005), 207.

2. Spiritual Bypassing and Shadow Work

1. Quoted in Tina Fossella, "Human Nature, Buddha Nature: An Interview with John Welwood," *Tricycle Magazine*, Spring 2011, https://tricycle.org/magazine/human-nature-buddha-nature/.

2. Quoted in Fossella, "Human Nature, Buddha Nature," https://tricycle.org/magazine/human-nature-buddha-nature/.

3. Quoted in Fossella, "Human Nature, Buddha Nature," https://tricycle.org/magazine/human-nature-buddha-nature/.

4. Belden Lane, *The Solace of Fierce Landscapes: Exploring Desert and Mountain Spirituality* (Oxford: Oxford University Press, 1998), 35.

5. Damon Garcia, *The God Who Riots: Taking Back the Radical Jesus* (Minneapolis, MN: Broadleaf Books, 2022), 83.

6. Rachel Ricketts, *Do Better: Spiritual Activism for Fighting and Healing from White Supremacy* (London: Gallery Book UK, 2021), 134–35.

7. Ricketts, *Do Better*, 136.

8. Mariana Caplan, *Eyes Wide Open: Cultivating Discernment on the Spiritual Path* (Boulder, CO: Sounds True, 2009), 140–41, Kindle.

9. Makoto Fujimura, *Art and Faith: A Theology of Making* (New Haven, CT: Yale University Press, 2021), 121.

10. Quoted in Fossella, "Human Nature, Buddha Nature," https://tricycle.org/magazine/human-nature-buddha-nature/.

11. Tracey Michae'l Lewis-Giggetts, *Then They Came for Mine: Healing from the Trauma of Racial Violence* (Louisville, KY: Westminster John Knox Press, 2022), 6.

12. Lewis-Giggetts, *Then They Came for Mine*, 12.

13. Rainer Maria Rilke, *Letters to a Young Poet*, trans. Stephen Mitchell (New York: Vintage Books, 2011), 23–24.

14. Miriam Greenspan, *Healing through the Dark Emotions: The Wisdom of Grief, Fear, and Despair* (Boulder, CO: Shambhala Publications, 2003).

15. Rumi, *The Essential Rumi*, trans. Coleman Barks (New York: HarperCollins, 1996), 109.

16. Benedict, "The Rule of Benedict," The Order of Saint Benedict, chapter 53. https://archive.osb.org/rb/text/rbeaad1.html#53.

17. Gregory Mayers, *Listen to the Desert: Secrets of Spiritual Maturity from the Desert Fathers and Mothers* (Barnhart, MO: Liguori Publications, 1996), 46–47.

18. Rumi, *Essential Rumi*, 109.

19. James Hollis, *Why Good People Do Bad Things: Understanding Our Darker Selves* (New York: Penguin, 2007), 9.

20. Barbara A. Holmes, *Joy Unspeakable: Contemplative Practices of the Black Church*, 2nd ed. (Minneapolis, MN: Fortress Press, 2017), 4.

21. Caplan, *Eyes Wide Open*, 184–85.

22. Caplan, *Eyes Wide Open*, 194.

23. Geneen Roth, *Women, Food, and God: An Unexpected Path to Almost Everything* (New York: Simon & Schuster, 2010), 92.

24. Roth, *Women, Food, and God*, 100.

25. Peter A. Levine, *In an Unspoken Voice: How the Body Releases Trauma and Restores Goodness* (Berkeley, CA: North Atlantic Books, 2010), xii.

26. Leticia Ochoa Adams, *Our Lady of Hot Messes: Getting Real with God in Dive Bars and Confessionals* (Notre Dame, IN: Ave Maria Press, 2022), 36.

3. GRIEF AS HOLY PATH

1. Francis Weller, *Entering the Healing Ground: Grief, Ritual and the Soul of the World* (Santa Rosa, CA: WisdomBridge Press, 2012), 18–19, Kindle.

2. Mary Oliver, *Winter Hours* (New York: Mariner Books, 1999), 106.

3. Weller, *Entering the Healing Ground*, 8.

4. Weller, *Entering the Healing Ground*, 122.

5. Clarissa Pinkola Estes, *Untie the Strong Woman* (Boulder, CO: Sounds True, 2011), 48.

6. Dietrich Bonhoeffer, *Letters and Papers from Prison* (New York: Touchstone Books, 1971), 176.

7. Mark Nepo, *The Book of Awakening* (Newburyport, MA: Red Wheel, 2020), 159.

8. Belden Lane, *The Solace of Fierce Landscapes: Exploring Desert and Mountain Spirituality* (Oxford: Oxford University Press, 1998), 73.

9. Denise Levertov, "The Love of Morning," in *Selected Poems*, ed. Paul Lacey (New York: New Directions, 2002), 166.

10. Michael Meade, "The Hidden Hope of the World," *Huffington Post*, updated October 11, 2011, https://www.huffpost.com/entry/america-crisis-hope_b_919452.

11. Cole Arthur Riley, *This Here Flesh: Spirituality, Liberation, and the Stories That Make Us* (New York: Convergent Books, 2022), 60.

12. Barbara Crooker, *Gold* (Eugene, OR: Cascade Books, 2013), 23. (Used by permission of Wipf and Stock Publishers, www.wipfandstock.com.)

4. THE APOPHATIC PATH OR WAY OF UNKNOWING

1. Gerald May, *The Dark Night of the Soul: A Psychiatrist Explores the Connection between Darkness and Spiritual Growth* (New York: HarperOne, 2009), 57.

2. May, *Dark Night of the Soul*, 72.

3. Richard Rohr, *The Naked Now: Learning to See as the Mystics See* (New York: Crossroad Publishing, 2013), 11–12.

4. Jean-Yves LeLoup, *Being Still: Reflections on an Ancient Mystical Tradition* (Mahwah, NJ: Paulist Press, 2003), 55.

5. Howard Thurman, *Meditations of the Heart* (Boston, MA: Beacon Press, 2014), 56–57.

6. Yolanda Pierce, *In My Grandmother's House: Black Women, Faith, and the Stories We Inherit* (Minneapolis, MN: Broadleaf Books, 2021), 49.

7. Constance FitzGerald, "Impasse and the Dark Night," Institute for Communal Contemplation and Dialogue, accessed March 14, 2024, https://iccdinstitute.org/impasse-and-dark-night/. Originally published in *Living with Apocalypse: Spiritual Resources for Social Compassion*, ed. Tilden H. Edwards, 93–116 (San Francisco: Harper & Row, 1984).

8. Dorothee Soelle, *Suffering* (Philadelphia: Fortress, 1975), 36.

9. Dennis O'Driscoll, "What She Does Not Know Is," *Collected Poems* (Manchester, England: Carcanet Press, 2017), 31. Reprinted by permission of Carcanet Press, UK.

5. THE COMPASSIONATE, FIERCE DARK FEMININE

1. Adapted from Christine Valters Paintner, *Birthing the Holy: Wisdom from Mary to Nurture Creativity and Renewal* (Notre Dame, IN: Sorin Books, 2022).

2. David Richo, *When Mary Becomes Cosmic: A Jungian and Mystical Path to the Divine Feminine* (Mahwah, NJ: Paulist Press, 2016), 26.

3. Christena Cleveland, *God Is a Black Woman* (New York: HarperOne, 2022), 56.

4. Demetra George, *Mysteries of the Dark Moon: The Healing Power of the Dark Goddess* (San Francisco: HarperCollins, 1994), 4.

5. Marion Woodman, *Dancing in the Flames: The Dark Goddess in the Transformation of Consciousness* (Boston, MA: Shambhala, 1996), 7.

6. Woodman, *Dancing in the Flames*, 16.

7. Sylvia Brinton Perera, *Descent to the Goddess: A Way of Initiation for Women* (Toronto, ON: Inner City Books, 1981), 36.

8. Diane Wolkstein and Samuel Noah Kramer, *Inanna, Queen of Heaven and Earth: Her Stories and Hymns from Sumer* (New York: Harper Perennial, 1983), 155.

9. Anselm of Canterbury, quoted in Vanessa R. Corcoran, "Five Years with the Virgin Mary: An Academic Pilgrimage by Dr. Vanessa Corcoran," *Today's American Catholic*, March 15, 2019, https://www.todaysamericancatholic.org/2019/03/five-years-with-the-virgin-mary-an-academic-pilgrimage/.

10. Vanessa R. Corcoran, "Queen of Heaven, Empress of Hell," *Contingent Magazine*, April 25, 2020, https://contingentmagazine.org/2020/04/25/empress-of-hell/.

6. The Transformative Mythic Journey

1. Excerpted and adapted from Christine Valters Paintner, *Illuminating the Way: Embracing the Wisdom of Monks and Mystics* (Notre Dame, IN: Sorin Books, 2016).

2. Carol Pearson, *Awakening the Heroes Within: Twelve Archetypes to Help Us Find Ourselves and Transform Our World* (San Francisco: HarperCollins, 1991), 139–40.

3. Pearson, *Awakening the Heroes Within*, 142.

4. Pearson, *Awakening the Heroes Within*, 143

5. Anita Barrows and Joanna Macy, *A Year with Rilke: Daily Readings from the Best of Rainer Maria Rilke* (San Francisco: HarperCollins, 2009), 6, Kindle.

6. James Hillman, *Re-Visioning Psychology* (New York: Harper-Collins, 1976), 207.

7. Robert Moore, *King, Warrior, Magician, and Lover* (San Francisco: HarperOne, 1991), 49.

8. Walter Wink, *The Human Being: Jesus and the Enigma of the Son of Man* (Minneapolis, MN: Augsburg Fortress, 2002), 154.

9. Excerpted and adapted from Christine Valters Paintner, *Illuminating the Way: Embracing the Wisdom of Monks and Mystics* (Notre Dame, IN: Sorin Books, 2016).

10. Christine Downing, *The Long Journey Home: Re-visioning the Myth of Demeter and Persephone for Our Time* (Boston, MA: Shambhala, 1994), 227.

11. Downing, *Long Journey Home*, 231.

12. Marion Woodman, *Addiction to Perfection: The Still Unravished Bride* (Toronto, ON: Inner City Books, 1982), 134.

13. Charles Stein, *Persephone Unveiled: Seeing the Goddess and Freeing Your Soul* (Berkeley, CA: North Atlantic Books, 2006), 89.

CONCLUSION

1. Belden Lane, *The Solace of Fierce Landscapes: Exploring Desert and Mountain Spirituality* (Oxford: Oxford University Press, 1998), 35.

2. Lane, *The Solace of Fierce Landscapes*, 20.

3. Ron Rolheiser, "Growth Through Dark Nights," Ron-Rolheiser.com, December 3, 2006, https://ronrolheiser.com/growth-through-dark-nights.

4. Christine Valters Paintner, "Let It Be Winter Still," in *Dreaming of Stones* (Brewster, MA: Paraclete Press, 2019), 40. Used by Permission of Paraclete Press. www.paracletepress.com.

Christine Valters Paintner is the online abbess for Abbey of the Arts, a virtual monastery offering classes and resources on contemplative practice and creative expression. She earned a doctorate in Christian spirituality from the Graduate Theological Union in Berkeley, California, and achieved professional status as a registered expressive arts consultant and educator from the International Expressive Arts Therapy Association. She is also trained as a spiritual director and supervisor.

Paintner is the author of numerous spirituality titles, including *The Love of Thousands*; *Birthing the Holy*; *Sacred Time*; *Earth, Our Original Monastery*; *The Soul's Slow Ripening*; *The Wisdom of the Body*; *Illuminating the Way*; *The Soul of a Pilgrim*; *The Artist's Rule*; *Water, Wind, Earth, and Fire*; and three collections of poetry.

She is a Benedictine oblate living in Galway, Ireland, with her husband, John. Together they lead online retreats at their website AbbeyoftheArts.com.

Facebook: @AbbeyoftheArts
Instagram: @abbeyofthearts
YouTube: www.youtube.com/@abbeyoftheartsireland

MORE BY
CHRISTINE VALTERS PAINTNER

Birthing the Holy
Wisdom from Mary to Nurture Creativity and Renewal

Earth, Our Original Monastery
Cultivating Wonder and Gratitude through Intimacy with Nature

Eyes of the Heart
Photography as a Christian Contemplative Practice

Illuminating the Way
Embracing the Wisdom of Monks and Mystics

Midwinter God
Encountering the Divine in Seasons of Darkness

Sacred Time
Embracing an Intentional Way of Life

The Artist's Rule
Nurturing Your Creative Soul with Monastic Wisdom

The Soul of a Pilgrim
Eight Practices for the Journey Within

The Soul's Slow Ripening
12 Celtic Practices for Seeking the Sacred

The Wisdom of the Body
A Contemplative Journey to Wholeness for Women

Water, Wind, Earth, and Fire
The Christian Practice of Praying with the Elements

Look for these titles wherever books and eBooks are sold.
Visit **avemariapress.com** to learn more.